The People's History

Beyond The Piers

A Tribute to the Fishermen of North Shields

by Ron Wright

A Grimsby registered trawler sets sail for the fishing grounds from the Tyne.

Previous page: Two men on a North Shields boat watch the Aberdeen registered *Ben Ardna*, which was a frequent visitor to the Tyne.

Copyright © Ron Wright 2002

First published in 2002 by

The People's History Ltd
Suite 1
Byron House
Seaham Grange Business Park
Seaham
Co. Durham
SR7 0PY

ISBN 1 902527 98 4

Contents

Introduction   5

1.   The Origins Of North Shields   9

2.   The Move From Sail To Steam   13

3.   Life Ashore   19

4.   Superstitions And The Wooden Dollies   29

5.   An Entrepreneur, Silver Fish And Tin Cans   35

6.   Jimmy's Story   43

7.   A Fisherman Allergic To Fish!   51

8.   No Thirty-Foot Waves On The River Tyne   55

9.   'What Was The Reason For Leaving Your Last Boat?' – 'Cos It Was Sinking'   61

10.   The Mysterious Loss Of The *Jeanie Stewart*   67

11.   Trawlers In The Wars   73

12.   The A To Z Of North Shields Registered Fishing Vessels, 1875-1967   85

Acknowledgements   124

Crewmembers of the SN 43 *St Gothard*.

This book is dedicated to the fisherman of North Shields and in particular to those who perished and whose unknown grave is the sea.

No wreaths can be laid where they rest, no hallowed ground can be visited to pay any respects.

Introduction

Fish and chips are an integral part of British life and many would identify them as the national dish yet few people consider the risks, the human endurance required to catch the fish and the human cost in lives over the years to provide such a nourishing and universally popular meal.

The fishing industry at North Shields came of age with the advent of steam, grew, prospered and died all within a time period of less than a century. The large steam trawling fleets have sailed into history and are in danger of being forgotten.

Forget about the romanticism which inevitably nostalgia brings, for it is always false. Life for the fisherman whether he was a deck hand or a skipper was hard, dangerous and was a test of an individual's endurance. The normal expectations of a civilised life such as sleep, warmth, dry clothing, sanitation, electricity and regular wages on board a trawler were invariably absent. The work was hard and the hours were long. He slept little, ate poorly, rarely washed and toilet facilities were at best basic. Life on board was all about catching fish, nothing else.

Life on board a steam trawler.

Imagine working for upwards of 14 days non-stop at sea and due to a poor catch actually finishing the trip in debt to the trawler owner. This happened, believe me, despite having worked a 100-hour week.

This book seeks to give the reader a taste of what life was like ashore and at sea during these vibrant and dynamic times and also serves to catalogue the fishing fleet of North Shields between 1875-1967. The period covered starts from the date that formal registration of all boats engaged in commercial fishing was enacted, through the rise and the fall of the age of steam, and up to the date of the withdrawal of the last steam trawler at North Shields which was SN 92 *Amerique* in 1967. By this time the vessel had been converted from coal to heavy oil but she still represented the last of the steam trawlers of North Shields.

Scant regard is paid to the rise of the diesel engined 'new age' fishing boats and some readers may consider that this is a failing. However, the age of steam correlates with the rise and subsequent demise of the deep sea fishing industry at North Shields, which was so important for the town and the community. Like many of the other great fishing ports such as Aberdeen, Grimsby and Hull the fishing industry at North Shields is now a shadow of its former self.

The glorious age of the steam drifter and trawler is over and the ships have all gone, most of them to the breakers yard but many of them to the cold murky depths of the sea. A typical steam trawler was a steel-built vessel, coal fired, 118 foot long with a 22-foot beam with storage space for between 60 to 70 tons of fish. The amount of space required for coal bunkerage and storage of fish was paramount and crew's quarters for 10 men were the bare minimum.

The men who sailed in them are now either approaching or are in the twilight of their lives. We need to remember them and their contribution.

Yet there was no shortage of men and boys at the quayside willing to sign on. One such man was Jimmy Cullen, who you will hear about later in the book. Once at sea the elements and the working conditions conspired to exacerbate their hard lives.

In 1910 the death rate on a trawler by accident and drowning was 1 in 203. Nothing among the shore industries, not even deep mining, could compete with these odds for mortality. But the industry was the only life hundreds of men and women knew at North Shields until it was killed off in the 1970s.

Now all that are left is memories. Men still talk in the pubs and clubs of the 'good old days', of standing watch in a force ten gale far out in the North Sea, of fishing around the clock with no sleep, of the friendship, and the feelings they encountered each and every time they saw the mouth of the River Tyne on their return home.

Dominating these memories are the steam trawlers themselves, long gone to the scrap yard except for SN 118 *Chris*, which in 1997 was in foreign ownership and seen berthed in Hamburg, Germany. It is believed that she is still afloat today. These trawlers were personal beings. They were not inanimate but lived and breathed. They had a

SN 118 *Chris*, seen in 1997 in Hamburg and believed to be still afloat.

definable character to the men who worked them. Even if two vessels had been built side by side by the same craftsmen, in the same shipyard from the same plans they would always be different to the trawler men. Almost always they were dirty, rusty, weather-beaten vessels, reeking of fish and the sea but like steam locomotives from the same era they acquired a romantic affection for those who worked them and for those who watched them from the safety of the shore.

It is hoped that these pages will appeal to maritime historians, local historians and people with a general interest in the sea and the fishing industry, its culture and the people who made it what it was.

Moreover it is a dedication to those people who brought fish to our tables and who genuinely are the salt of the earth, no pun intended!

Ron Wright
Cullercoats, 2002

Peter Forster and his crewmates prepare to leave North Shields Fish Quay on another trip.

THE ORIGINS OF NORTH SHIELDS

A busy day at the Fish Quay by the Low Lights.

The name of Shields is derived from the name given to the fishermen's huts or 'shiels' which were the earliest dwellings alongside the river. By the end of the 14th century the name North Shields was being used to distinguish it from a similar town across the river.

The history of North Shields and its association with the fishing industry is inextricably linked to the birth of Christianity in the region and with the building of Tynemouth Priory at the end of the 11th century. This monastic patronage and the struggle with Newcastle dominated the rise and fall and rise of North Shields over many centuries.

North Shields did not exist at this time but by the early part of the 13th century the monks from the priory began developing the town of North Shields, which sat outside the monastic defences.

In 1225, Prior Germanes of Tynemouth Priory and the monks drained and reclaimed a large portion of the marshland near the mouth of the river and created North Shields. This township of 27 houses with quays quickly became a thriving community of 100 houses with wharfs, mills and quays, which established a salt, hide, fishing and coal industry. Within a short space of time the town was inhabited by 1000 people who lived in thatched-roofed houses along the banks of the River Tyne.

However, the creation of North Shields did not find favour with the Burgesses of the Royal Borough of Newcastle who viewed North Shields as a threat to their business interests. In retribution, and in an effort to stifle the growth of North Shields, the mayor and an armed rabble from Newcastle sacked the town in 1270. Houses and mills were burned. The monastery responded by way of a lawsuit against Newcastle, which allowed North Shields to prosper once again.

Then in 1290 the Newcastle Burgesses obtained parliamentary sanction to destroy North Shields in order to protect the monopoly of trade that Newcastle wished to continue. Owners of vessels were forbidden to load or unload at North Shields, the victualling of merchantmen was banned and the wharfs were destroyed. North Shields sank into the doldrums for the next century.

However, the monks and the townspeople of North Shields were obviously made of sterner stuff and by 1429, and despite further attempts by the merchants of Newcastle to thwart the ambitions of 'shiels folk', a settlement of 200 houses and 14 fish quays stood where North Shields stands today. Fish from as far away as Iceland was being landed at North Shields by this time.

The fortunes of North Shields continued to ebb and flow like the incessant tide but by the 18th century the harbour and river at North Shields was alive with commerce, the main activities being the landing of fish and the export of coal together with shipbuilding. By 1820 the fishing industry established at the port had progressed sufficiently to warrant the building of a fish market.

The arrival of the industrial age, the birth of the railways, the nearness of an abundant and cheap coal supply and the use of steam to

The Fish Quay and the Low Lights, *circa* 1880.

propel fishing vessels created the town of North Shields as it is known today.

The town began to grow upwards away from the banks of the River Tyne. Prior to this North Shields was in effect Low Street. However, prosperous shipowners built houses above the banks in Dockwray Square where they had a commanding view of the river and the harbour. Toll Square and Tyne Terrace quickly followed for the shipowners and shipbuilders.

But for the working class the majority continued to live in the narrow, crowded, squalid, tenement streets off Low Street and the many streets of different names that ran off it. All the main businesses of the town were housed in this area, which included 50 public houses within the stretch of a quarter mile.

In 1849, through the enactment of Royal Charter of Incorporation, the Municipal Borough of Tynemouth was created incorporating Tynemouth, North Shields, Chirton, Preston and Cullercoats. The motto for the Borough that highlighted the two main reasons for the town's prosperity became:

'Messis ab Altis' – 'Our harvest is from the deep.'

The Royal Coat of Arms for Tynemouth depicts three crowns and above the shield is a ship and on one side a sailor and on the other side a miner. The three crowns are reputed to represent the three kings that were buried in the Tynemouth Priory. They were King Osred of Northumberland, St Oswin who was born in South Shields and Malcolm III, King of Scotland, who was slain at the Battle of Alnwick in 1093.

In 1870 the foundations of the current fish quay was constructed which has been added to and refurbished over the last 130 years.

A quiet day at the Fish Quay awaiting the return of the trawlers and drifters.

THE MOVE FROM SAIL TO STEAM

How it all started. A steam paddle tug with a sailing trawler in tow.

Fish Quay, *circa* 1880.

During the 1860s the fishing fleet of North Shields comprised of sailing smacks and luggers. Steam-powered paddle tugs had made their mark by this time and were frequently employed to give the sailing smacks and luggers a pull out of harbour when the wind conditions made it impossible for them to sail out. These steam tugs, all of which were at this time paddle driven, were powerful beasts and it was not unknown for them to cross the North Sea to ports such as Amsterdam and tow large sailing ships back to the River Tyne when the winds prevented them from making the passage eastwards.

In 1868 the paddle tug *Castrina* sailed to Gibraltar, without towage, from the River Tyne in three days and three hours. Tugs were recorded as towing sailing ships from Liverpool to the River Clyde in thirty hours despite gale force winds.

The business of steam towage on the River Tyne was fickle and the arrival of sailing ships unpredictable. The owners of the steam paddle tugs were constantly searching for work in the North Sea but many of the tugs were laid up with nothing to do.

In 1873 there were 145 steam tugs alone registered on the River Tyne so it can be appreciated, busy though the river was at this time, that competition was fierce and the returns small.

In November 1877 a sailing smack of 50 tons gross called the *Zenith* and registered as SN 944 became becalmed off the mouth of the River

Tyne having shot her trawl. The skipper, James Kelly, reputedly a native of Hull, requested the tug *Messenger*, captained by William Purdy, to tow him into harbour. The trawl was left down. It is reported that the *Zenith* landed a good catch of fish in excess of that which was anticipated. It was this experience that prompted Purdy to wonder at the logic of towing a trawl himself. No doubt prompted by the lean times Purdy fitted-out the *Messenger* with second-hand trawl nets and gear, much to the derision of the local smacksmen and luggermen. The trawling equipment made up of gear sourced from Grimsby, North Shields and Sunderland cost a total of £19 10 shillings, plus the installation of a small derrick.

On 2nd November 1877 Purdy, together with two crew members Thomas Tomlinson and a man called Fryall, left the North Shields Fish Quay on his maiden fishing trip to cries of ridicule about him wasting his money and that his venture was bound to fail. Jeers and catcalls abounded together with the throwing of rotten fruit as they sailed away from the quay.

Within two voyages the prophets of failure were silenced. His first voyage netted a catch worth £7 10 shillings plus an additional £5 for towage of a sailing ship into the River Tyne and upon his return from his second voyage Purdy had made a modest profit but he had proved his point. Purdy quickly capitalised on his achievement by declaring on his billheads:

'William Purdy of North Shields. Pioneer of Steam Trawling 1877.'

Paddle Tugs moored by the Fish Quay, many of these were used as trawlers.

There followed a rush to fit-out unemployed paddle tugs with beam trawls. The *Messenger*, which never bore a SN fishing registration, was quickly joined by SN 1083 *Pilot*, SN 1089 *Conquest*, SN 1112/1412 *Patriot* (registered twice at North Shields) and many others until there was not an idle tug left at the moorings.

The example of North Shields was quickly followed by other ports up and down the North East coast and Scotland and within a year 50 paddle tug masters had followed Purdy's example. Steam in the fishing industry had come of age and had proved that it could catch fish.

The face of the fishing industry was changed. The rush to put paddle tugs into service as trawlers was not without its problems. These old wooden vessels were not fit for the daily grind of towing a heavy beam trawl along the seabed. The attrition rate was high. In the first six months of 1880 eight tugs converted for trawling were lost.

Now larger steam paddlers built of wood and iron were specially constructed for trawling but this form of propulsion only lasted a short period. Paddlers, whilst at home on the inshore grounds, were unsuitable for the turbulent seas around the Dogger Bank and beyond. Thoughts turned to the propeller as a more efficient means of propulsion. However, Scarborough remained faithful to the steam paddlers until 1904 when the last of the paddlers SH 1237 *Hartland*, formerly registered as SN 1516, ceased fishing.

Steam trawlers jostling for position at North Shields Fish Quay.

The first steam screw trawler appeared at North Shields in 1881 as SN 1168 *Bonito* but she had left the North Shields registry by 1887. Throughout the fishing industry the screw steam trawler proliferated especially in the North Eastern ports where coal was in abundance and the coalfields were only a short distance away. Cheap coal in abundance was reflected in cheap fish in abundance. The railway lines, which carried the coal to the fish docks, transported the fish to the inland industrial towns.

Noel Coward could well have coined the phrase:

'they caught the cod that fed the miners that dug the coal that powered the ships that caught the cod that …'

The application of steam powered engines to propel fishing vessels came surprisingly late in the 1800s and not without its fair share of sceptics. Whilst the British Isles were covered with a network of steam railways during the reign of Queen Victoria this new form of motive power was much slower in reaching the fishing fleets. Yet North Shields was at the forefront of this change and the man who is credited with the introduction and application of steam to trawl fishing is William Purdy, a native of the town.

Steam was slower in coming to the smaller drifters but was no less inevitable. The first registered steam drifter is believed to have been the SN 1492 *Pioneer*.

Trawlers and drifters fish for different fish and in a different way. Trawlers seek to catch demersal or bottom-feeding fish such as cod, haddock, plaice, sole, skate, turbot, brill and halibut. The trawl net is towed behind a single vessel and is dragged along the bottom of the seabed. A beam holds open the net that gradually diminishes in size and the fish are trapped towards the end of the net which is like an elongated triangle.

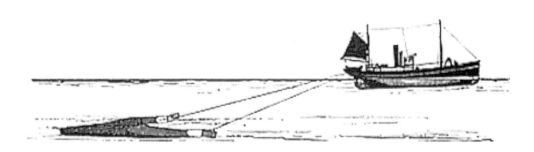

A diagram of trawler towing a trawl along the bottom of the sea bed.

Drifters, however, search for pelagic fish such as herring, sprats, mackerel and pilchards. These fish swim close to the surface of the sea and are caught by means of a drift net that hangs down in the water like a weighted curtain and traps the fish by their gills.

The explosion in the birth of the steam screw trawler brought further benefits to North Shields and its surrounding area - that of building the vessels. The shipyards on the River Tyne turned them out at an amazing rate. It was not unknown for a steam trawler to be built from keel to maiden voyage in less than forty days. Small yards, now long defunct, such as the Union Co-operative Shipbuilding Society at Cowpen Square, Blyth turned out nine ninety-ton trawler/drifters in a three-year period.

By 1904 the port of North Shields was in its heyday with registrations of first class vessels at a high of 143 – 135 of which were steam driven.

Sixty years later total registrations had collapsed to only twenty two, only one of which was a steam trawler.

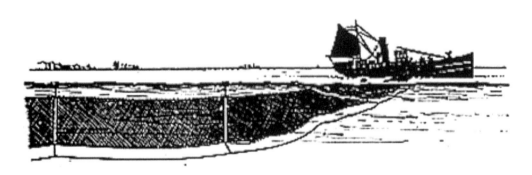

Above: A diagram of a steam drifter shooting her nets. *Below*: Once shot, the boat swings around and lies with her nets like a curtain along the surface to catch the fish.

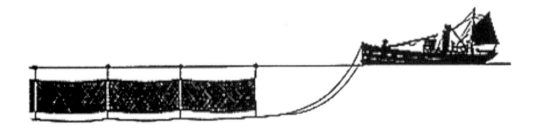

LIFE ASHORE

Low Street, *circa* 1930s – where many of the fishermen lived.

The rich and poor on the Fish Quay.

If life was hard and tough for the fishermen at sea, certainly for the first 50 years of the 20th century, life for many was little better ashore. The romanticised vision of the fishermen as a simple and kindly soul in a souwester, smoking a pipe whilst sat on a barrel in a cobbled street did not exist. The truth was very different.

The housing conditions along the Fish Quay were dingy and squalid with poor basic amenities. Fish was in abundance and very cheap. It is estimated that in 1914 there were in excess of 20,000 fish and chip shops spread across England which provided cheap meals for many of the inhabitants who had only rudimentary cooking facilities, if they had any at all. Fish and chips were not a luxury but for many the stable diet. George Orwell wrote in his book *The Road to Wigan Pier*, 'You can't get much meat for three pence ($1^1/_2$ new pence) but you can get a lot of fish and chips.'

Fishermen were poorly rewarded and often exploited during the time that the industry developed, prospered and eventually failed.

A fishermen's wages depended entirely upon the success of the catch and at the start of the 20th century in many cases no basic wage was received. His remuneration by way of wages was in the hands of the trawler owner; it depended upon the skill of the skipper in finding large quantities of fish and finally was at the mercy of the vagrancies of the fish market.

At this time the value of the catch was divided as follows – 50% of the value of the catch automatically went to the trawler owner and the remainder formed the basis for the wages. However, this amount of

Where the Rich and the Working Class Lived

Dockwray Square, *circa* 1890 – where the shipowners and businessmen lived.

Bell Street Quay, *circa* 1914 – the home for many poor families.

Inside 69 Clive Street around the 1930s.

Not much luxury ashore.

money was a net amount after the cost of the fuel, coal, ice, food for the trip, net repairs and breakages had been deducted.

As the food, coal and ice was provided by the trawler owner through his own outlets, the exploitation of these costs in the trawler owner's favour was always a possibility and more likely to be a probability. It was then at this point that the crew could be paid – 10 to 15% of the money remaining was paid to the skipper and the final remaining amount was divided on a share basis amongst the crew according to prior agreement. This was known as the 'settling' and was later known as the 'poundage'.

A copy of a 'settling' from the Purdy owned trawler, SN 129
Edith M Purdy, in 1953.

Whilst at sea the wife of a crew member could draw an advance on her husband's wages known as a 'sub' which would then have to be repaid to the trawler owner at the time of the settling. If the trip had been a poor one the advance drawn by a crew member's wife could be, and was in many cases, in excess of a crew member's settling. He then 'settled in debt' to the trawler owner and this debt was carried over to the next trip when he hoped for a decent catch.

A series of changes followed and by 1928 through the Fishing Vessels Owners' Associations a general standard of conditions was published, although the possibility of exploitation by the trawler owner was still possible.

The skipper and mate were not paid a basic wage but a percentage of the net earnings of a boat. The remaining crewmembers received a

All classes of residents could be seen on the Fish Quay.

basic wage with some benefits if they had a good catch. The wages are detailed below.

Skipper – One and three-eighths of fourteen shares of the net earnings plus a bonus of £50 for gross amounts of £8,000 per annum plus an additional £1 for every £100 in excess of £8,000. Any days where the skipper was required on board whilst the vessel was docked he was paid eight shillings per day (40 new pence).

Mate – One and one-eighth of fourteen shares of the net earnings of the vessel. He received no bonus and if required to be on board whilst the vessel was docked he was paid seven shillings per day (35 new pence).

Chief Engineer – A basic wage of thirteen shillings and sixpence per week sea pay (67$\frac{1}{2}$ new pence) and ten shillings per week (50 pence) harbour pay.

Second Engineer – A basic wage of twelve shillings per day sea pay (60 new pence) and eight shillings and sixpence (42$\frac{1}{2}$ new pence) harbour pay.

Third Hand, Deckhand, Fireman and Cook – A basic wage of eight shillings and sixpence (42$\frac{1}{2}$ new pence) sea pay and six shillings (30 new pence) harbour pay. In addition to the basic wage the third hand if he was a net mender received an additional three pence (1$\frac{1}{2}$ new pence) or two pence (one new pence) if he was not a net mender for every £1 in value of fish landed. The remaining crewmembers received a further one pence ($\frac{1}{2}$ new pence) for every £1 in value of fish landed.

Finally each crewmember was allowed a fry of fish, the value of which was not to exceed three shillings (fifteen new pence). The crew were strictly forbidden to give the fish away and the River and Tynemouth Borough Police were instructed to apprehend any person either giving or receiving a fry of fish.

A clear day without pay was allowed at the end of each settling of eleven days or more. Vessels landing on the Saturday were required to return to sea on the following Monday.

By the time that Purdy first proved that steam trawling was possible and profitable and with the rewards that steam trawling brought to the trawler owners, North Shields and Tynemouth Borough developed beyond all recognition. Whilst the Low Town of North Shields was still a densely populated slum the main streets and residential areas of North Shields and Tynemouth had been built and remain in the same form to this day. The main streets were paved and lighted but it was not until well into the 20th century that the slums of the Low Town were demolished.

It is not surprising that many fishermen chose to spend most of their time ashore in the inns and pubs of North Shields, of which there was abundance.

Fishermen always portrayed an image of being well off and able to spend extravagantly as they often did in port. But irrespective of whether they had had a good, bad or indifferent trip the fact remained that they still had only two days ashore to spend what had probably been earned in three weeks. There is no use for money at sea.

Preparing fish for the Market.

Scots fisher lasses who used to follow the herring fleet from port to port.

Ogilvy's Leyland lorry – one of the first lorries on the Fish Quay.

In 1854 there were 183 public houses in the Royal Borough of Tynemouth, almost all of them in the Low Town of North Shields. The population at this time stood at 14,483 giving a ratio of a pub for every 79 residents. By 1901 there remained over 140 licensed pubs and most of them in the Low Town were dens of inequity. An examination of the Licensing Victuallers register for a five year period at the beginning of the 1900s shows that almost all of the landlords had been cited for various offences, the most prevalent offences being:

Supplying intoxication liquor to a habitual drunkard.
Adulteration of Whisky – ie watering it down.
Refusing to admit the Police.
Supplying the police with alcoholic liquor – obviously this publican let them in!
Supplying intoxicating liquor to a minor under the age of 14 years.
Allowing the playing of billiards on a Christian day.
Allowing prostitutes to remain on the premises longer than necessary – how long do they consider is reasonable?
Harbouring prostitutes.

The main areas where the pubs were situated was along the main road through the Low Town covering Duke Street, Clive Street, Liddell Street, Bell Street and Union Quay through to the Low Lights. These streets are still there to be seen today but alas the vast majority of the pubs have long gone. In 1854 Duke Street ran from where the North Shields Metro Ferry docks to the bottom of Borough Bank, a distance of little more than 100 yards. No less than seven pubs occupied this short street and two of them are still there to be seen and enjoyed. The Crane House is now known as the Chainlocker and the Golden Fleece has been renamed the Porthole. Continuing eastwards towards the Fish

The Newcastle Arms and Lord Collingwood.

Quay, Clive Street ran from the bottom of Borough Bank to the bottom of Bedford Street, a distance of little more than 300 yards. Eighteen pubs vied for business here but none remain today.

Liddell Street continues towards the Fish Quay from the new Dolphin Quay complex to the Ice Factory. Ten more pubs occupied this short distance and the Prince of Wales remains there today. The North Shields Fish Quay now opens out before you, covering Bell Street, the Union Quay and the Low Lights. This area was serviced by a further 52 pubs but only two of these buildings remain today which were there in 1854. These pubs are the Highlander Hotel, which is now William Wight's Grocers, and the Low Lights Tavern at the end of the Fish Quay. The New Dolphin Inn is a comparatively newcomer at just 100 years old.

In 1878 the police reported that they had dealt with 914 persons for offences of drunkenness and disorderly conduct. This was actually a 50% reduction over those arrested in 1873 and the report details that they had dealt with 158 thieves, 157 vagrants, 301 prostitutes and 682 habitual drunkards. The vast majority of these offenders had been apprehended in the Low Town.

In 1883 it was found necessary to build a second major police station in the Bull Ring of the Low Town to police this heavily populated area to 'prevent many a disgraceful scene in the street such as often occurred, the largest majority of prisoners are locked up from that part of the town.' This police station eventually closed in 1925.

Bad weather and bad seas exacerbate a hard and physical job. The North Sea is a cold and hostile environment and the fishermen on deck were exposed to snow, ice, wind and rain. Despite what the elements threw at them the work had to go on. The fish were unaffected by the conditions and were there to be taken.

Keens, blisters and wounds had to be ignored. Fishermen would urinate on their hands to allow the ammonia in their urine to clean and heal their wounds. It is known that they would resort to sealing their wounds with hot tar. Is it any wonder that they drowned their sorrows in the warm and welcoming pubs of the Low Town?

Has a fishwife fallen foul of the Law?

North Shields Police, *circa* 1912.

SUPERSTITIONS AND
THE WOODEN DOLLIES

Wooden Dolly No 6, situated where
all of the Wooden Dollies have stood
except one.

The buxom Wooden Dolly No 3 looking towards the Fish Quay.

North Shields heritage is firmly anchored in the sea but a fisherman's battle with nature is dominated with adherence to superstition. All seafarers are superstitious but there are none more superstitious than fishermen.

On the day of sailing fishermen, once they had left home, would not look back or turn back. Meeting a clergyman or a nun on the way to the boat spelt bad luck. It is reputed that it is written in some conditions of service that if such an eventuality arose the fisherman could rightly refuse to go to sea. Seeing a pig was infinitely worse.

Their womenfolk were also bound by superstition. They were not allowed to wash clothes on the day of a sailing lest their men 'be washed overboard.' Once he had left home they were not allowed to call after him or go down to the dock to see him off. Whistling was taboo as it might 'whistle up a storm.'

Green was considered to be an unlucky colour both on shore and at sea. Houses were not painted green and trawlers never so. Green clothing was not allowed and any fishermen wearing an item of green clothing (such as an apprentice deckie) was likely to have the offending item torn off his back and thrown overboard. No experienced fishermen would ever wear green.

The superstitions continued once at sea. Friday was a day to be avoided to start a trip. Words such as pig, rabbit, monkey, salt and rat were never uttered at sea.

Why these words were taboo is lost in the annals of history and folklore. The word pig could not be used but instead grunter or something similar was acceptable. Should any of these taboo words be used by anyone when preparation for fishing were going forward then some ill luck would follow, such as lost nets or lines or a poor catch. If a stranger inadvertently mentioned such a word the impending ill luck could be averted by either grasping cold iron or turning your cap around on your head a full 360 degrees.

Fishermen's big sea boots were always carried one under each arm with their toes pointing forward. To carry sea boots together with the toes pointing downwards held that the owner would be carried home drowned before the night was over.

For nearly 200 years a series of Wooden Dollies have adorned the Fish Quay and they quickly became part of local folklore. Despite their perceived magical properties they were badly treated. The Dollies fastened themselves in people's memory and imagination and an ex-native of North Shields when meeting one of his kinsfolk was likely to ask after the Wooden Dolly.

> For many years she stood upon the Fish Quay
> A problematical symbol of the past
> The figurehead of some forgotten trader
> She had travelled many miles before the mast.
>
> And everyone paid to homage to the lady
> She was worshipped by the seamen's brotherhood
> Amazing when you think that she was only
> An ordinary Dolly made of wood.
>
> They came from every corner of the nation
> Like pilgrims on their journey to a shrine
> And they gathered there in silent acclamation
> Round the Dolly on the North side of the Tyne.
>
> Now the Wooden Dolly was famous but unhappy
> She was mugged by cruel vandals through the years
> They chipped large lumps of wood from her person
> And they carried them away for souvenirs.

This portion of a poem by Jack Davitt (aka Ripyard Cuddling) encapsulates the spirit of the Wooden Dollies.

No photographs or sketches are known to exist of the first Wooden Dolly, which was the figurehead of a collier brig named the *Alexander and Margaret*. This North Shields collier was captured off Great Yarmouth by the pirate William Fall and in the desperate one-sided battle to save his ship the captain of the *Alexander and Margaret*, David Bartleman, who was also the son of the ship's owner was mortally wounded. As a mark of respect the figurehead – Wooden Dolly No 1 – was placed at the entrance to Custom House Quay in 1814. There she resided until 1850 when she was vandalised and decapitated by the loutish behaviour of some Saturday night drunks.

Wooden Dolly No 2 was another ship's figurehead and she was erected in the same location in 1850. Little is known of this Dolly. She belonged to Mr Hare, a sailmaker, on Custom House Quay and she remained in situ for 14 years until she was replaced. Unfortunately no photographs or sketches are known to exist of Wooden Dolly No 2.

Wooden Dolly No 3 was also a ship's figurehead from the barque *Expert* owned by Peter and John Stephenson. This was no slim, simpering goddess-like creature from a Greek frieze but a buxom, comely wench with a shapely figure with a full flaunty petticoat. By now the Wooden Dolly had made her mark and was seen as a good luck talisman for seafaring men. She occupied the same position on Custom House Quay as her predecessors and the area was under her influence. Custom House Quay became known as Wooden Dolly Quay; the Custom House steps became the Wooden Dolly Steps; and the nearby Prince of Wales public house became known as the Wooden Dolly public house. The public house is still there today and continues to bear this dual identity.

Wooden Dolly No 3, 1864-1901.

Wooden Dolly No 4, 1902-57.

Wooden Dolly No 4, shortly before replacement.

Whilst standing proudly on the Quay, Wooden Dolly No 3 suffered a similar fate to those whom had gone before her. Seafarers chipped pieces from the Dolly to carry with them all over the world for good luck. Constant repair, including a new nose, kept her alive until 1901 when she was replaced. However, Wooden Dolly No 3 may still be with us. Seventy years after she was replaced she surfaced in the possession of a Newcastle antique dealer, where she had languished for many years, after she had been bought from a fisherman. She was still a formidable sight despite being unloved and unwanted. Her nose was missing again and no paint remained on her body. Wooden Dolly No 3 is believed to be somewhere in Denmark today.

Wooden Dolly No 4 broke with tradition and was not a figurehead from a ship. She was a commissioned carving by May Spence of North Shields. This Wooden Dolly depicted a stooped fishwife with a creel on her back. This was a controversial Dolly and the sculptress wanted a local shipowner, James Knott, to perform the unveiling ceremony. The councillors of the day, however, did not consider Knott to be a local man, after all he had been born in Howdon and now resided outside of the Borough, so a local councillor took the honour. Wooden Dolly No 4 survived for over half a century before she too became so mutilated that she had to be replaced.

Wooden Dolly No 5 like Wooden Dolly No 4 broke with a tradition going back 144 years. Although she too is a fishwife, carved in the likeness of May Spence's Wooden Dolly, she stands in Northumberland Square, North Shields, far from the Fish Quay. Erected in 1958 she still stands there today but no seafarers pay homage to her.

A sixth wooden dolly – Wooden Dolly No 6 – now stands where Wooden Dollies Nos 1, 2, 3 and 4 once stood. Erected in 1992 she is carved out of a solid piece of oak and is based on Wooden Dolly No 3. This Wooden Dolly continues the original tradition but sadly there are few seafarers left to ask for her favour of a safe passage.

The Wooden Dollies of the Fish Quay presided over a period of immense change in the fortunes of North Shields. They witnessed the rise and fall of the fishing industry; the decline of the sailing ship; the period when Low Street was the busiest commercial street in North Shields; and the rise and development of the steamship and steam trawler.

It is hoped that Wooden Dolly No 6 will remain as a landmark or a reminder of the colourful history of North Shields.

Wooden Dolly No 5.

An Entrepreneur, Silver Fish And Tin Cans

An advertisement for Tyne Brand herrings –
'Packed fresh – Always fresh.'

If North Shields is proud of the fact that one of their own, William Purdy, recognised and put into practice the application of steam power to the fishing industry no account of this success would be complete without also recognising the contribution of Richard Irvin.

Richard Irvin was born of humble origins in North Shields in 1858 and by the time he was 16 years old he was a marine store dealer. Three years later he was the part owner of a sailing trawler called the *Zenith*. It is not known whether it was this trawler that Purdy towed into the Tyne with his tug the *Messenger* setting the trend to move to steam power but Irvin recognised the benefits and was soon the owner of his first steam trawler, the *Enterprise*.

Irvin was never short of enterprise and business acumen and in 1890 he realised that Aberdeen was destined to become a leading fishing port and opened his first branch office there. This marked the start of many such ventures.

In 1901 Irvin built and opened the Shields Ice and Cold Storage Company to supplement the ice making facilities on the Fish Quay. By this time he owned thirteen North Shields registered steam drifters and trawlers and no doubt had part shares in many other boats.

Always eager to expand his business interests Irvin recognised that there was an over abundance of fish being landed which was outstripping demand. Large quantities of prime haddock were being sold to the local guano factory to make fertilizer. Seizing upon the

Drifters waiting to land their catch of herring, much of it destined to be canned by Tyne Brand.

Fish on the Quay waiting for the auction.

opportunity he expanded the facilities of the Shields Ice and Cold
Storage Company to create a cannery and started to can haddock. For
once he got it wrong. Canned haddock was not popular so he swiftly
switched to herring, which was being caught in copious amounts, and
he never looked back.

By 1913, only forty years after he purchased his first sailing trawler,
Irvin was head of a huge business, the largest of its kind in the world.
Branch offices and agents of the company were now in the ports of
Aberdeen, Great Yarmouth, Lowestoft, Peterhead. Blyth, Lerwick,
Stornaway, Castlebay, Mallaig, Downings Bay, Milford Haven as well as
North Shields. Fifty steam trawlers and drifters were owned by his
company and he had a controlling interest in a further seventy fishing
vessels. He had also by this time become the owner of the Shields
Engineering and Dry Dock, colloquially known as the 'Haddock Shop'.
The original dry dock can still be seen by the edge of the Dolphin
Quays housing complex which now occupies the site.

However, Irvin did not just confine himself to home shores. He had
significant business interests in the African Fishing and Trading
Company and Irvin and Johnson's Ltd in South Africa with offices in
Cape Town, Durban, Johannesburg, Port Elizabeth and Bloomfontain.
Many North Shields trawlers ended up in the warm waters off the
South African coast.

Not content with his African interests, Irvin moved across the
Atlantic where he was Chairman of the Southern Whaling and Sealing
Company, a company with stations on South Georgia, the Falkland

From these three Tyne Brand factories, Tynemouth despatches quality food products all over the world.

Now one of the leading canners of food products — the name TYNE BRAND has become a household word for quality foods. Sold everywhere throughout the British Isles and distributed throughout the world. During the late war the Company supplied no less than 130 million cans of various foods to H.M. Services.

The Tyne Brand Range Herrings In Tomato Sauce. Fresh Herrings. Kippers. Herring Roes. Cod Roes. Haddocks. Etc., etc. Fish and Meat Pastes (in glasses and tins). Tomato Ketchup. Chutney. French Mustard. Horseradinh Sauces, etc. Mint Sauce. "So-Taist-Ee" Extract. Canned Fruit and Vegetables. Soups. Puddings. Meat Roll, and a large variety of prepared canned meats and ready meals.

An advertisement showing the Tyne Brand factory.

Islands, Port Alexander, Portuguese West Africa and the Marion and Prince Edward Islands.

How Richard Irvin managed to control such a diverse business empire without the benefit of facsimile machines, e-mail and a rapid air transport system is a source of wonderment.

This Victorian entrepreneur, however, remained firmly rooted in North Shields where he had created a monopoly of companies which made and repaired the trawlers, owned the trawlers, supplied the ice for the trawlers, caught the fish, sold the fish at the market and canned the fish for consumption around the world.

Richard Irvin must have been an outstanding personality. Many of the people of North Shields may not remember Richard Irvin but most have memories of one of his successes – Tyne Brand. Tyne Brand was the trade name used for the products canned by the Shields Ice and Cold Storage Company which was later to be renamed Tyne Brand.

Nowadays canned food, freeze dried food and frozen food is such a part of everyday life that it is difficult to envisage how canned herring in tomatoes sauce under the Tyne Brand name became so significant and such a major part of North Shields life. For a period other food products were canned such as: Salmon; Ox Tongue; Chicken Breast in Jelly; Roast Chicken; Roast Goose; Boneless Turkey; Mustard; Tomato Ketchup; Olive Oil; Meat Brawn; Jellied Veal; Pâté; Chicken, Ham and Tongue Roll; Meat and Fish pastes and Fish Cakes in tins – but the Tyne Brand Herring in Tomato Sauce reined supreme.

In 1927 Tyne Brand rationalised their products into three fish products concentrating on the herring.

Five hundred years ago the greater part of the inland population would never see a fish caught in the sea. One hundred years ago their were still many who still had not eaten a fresh sea fish.

Refrigeration and salting kept the fish in edible condition but at a price. Smoking and drying changed the character of the fish so completely that the herring, the most prolific fish on the English and Scottish seaboard, even changed in name. Split and smoked it became the kipper, smoked whole it became a bloater. As a fresh herring it appeared in quantity on the fishmonger's slab only for a few months of the year.

Canning allowed the regular of supply of prime fish irrespective of uneven catches, bad weather or the season of the year. Canning also liberated the housewife from the drudgery of preparing and cooking fish for the table.

Everyone wants to see how the catch has been.

Herring, especially those caught in the summer months, are richer in vitamins and food value pound for pound than beef or eggs. Their natural oils are beneficial and the bones – edible after canning – are good for the brain. And they were cheap!

Let me attempt to set the scene for a typical North Shields day, which Richard Irvin must have delighted in, between June and August.

At this time the migrating shoals of herring are off the North East coast and are at their prime as they feed on the rich summer plankton. Herring move in shoals around the coast of Great Britain in a clockwise direction starting in the far North East of Scotland and ending in late autumn off the South West of England.

Herrings are caught by drifters and unlike their bigger sisters, the trawlers, which go to sea for weeks on end, a drifter, will generally stay out only for one night. Each afternoon the grimy, rusting, smoking, but sea worthy drifters, set sail from the Tyne seeking the herring shoals. Each one hoped for a good catch – a catch that would allow them back to port in time to get the best price. Fishing takes place throughout the night and then it is full speed back to Shields.

The sun rises early at this time of year and as dawn breaks the first of the drifters are back in port. The misty morning is made worse by the drifters as they choke in the smoke of each other's funnels.

Salting and casking the herring – the girl in the middle looking at the camera is from North Shields.

Buskers, freshers, canners, kipperers and curers passing the time away.

The quayside is lively with blue jerseyed fisher folk, Scots lassies knitting beside empty casks, small boys, tourists and men in business dress. The blue jerseyed ones are 'buskers' who are there in search of casual labour. The Scots lasses are there to gut and salt down the herrings in casks for the 'curers'. These girls are like the herring. They migrate around the country following the herring, working in each port where they are well respected for their hard work and skill. Whilst waiting for the boats to land their catches they knit heavy wool jumpers, which they sell to the fishermen.

The small boys are there to pick up any herrings which fall from the baskets as they are unloaded. The men in the business suits are the 'freshers', 'curers', 'kipperers' and the 'canners' who will shortly bid against each other for the catch. As soon as the drifters touch the quayside a sample of their catch is taken to the 'ring', the auction floor, where the buyers gather for the sale. If all the drifters bring in good catches the price is low. Luck is in for the drifter which brings in a good catch when supplies are short.

The canners are looking for herring which are 3-4 years old and in their prime. If the herring's age is right, the samples are fair and the fish plump then the deal is done. The fish are on their way to the canners from the quayside whilst the last of the drifters are putting into harbour.

Once at the Tyne Brand cannery the fish are gutted, beheaded, cleaned and washed.

Now they are arranged in the cans on a bed of tomato sauce, top and tailed. The cans are specifically designed to prevent damage to the fish during packing. The tops of the cans are clinched on and the cans passed through steam-heated exhausts, which ensures that all air is removed from the cans. The cans are then firmly sealed and the contents cooked in huge steel ovens heated by dry steam. The cooking preserves the fish in the can and ensures that it is kept in perfect condition.

The cans are stacked in a warehouse to mature and then finally labelled with the Tyne Brand slogan: 'Packed fresh – Always fresh.'

In its heyday 3,000,000,000 herrings were netted off the English and Scottish coasts in an average season, many of them destined to be canned by Tyne Brand.

In 1961 Tyne Brand Herrings ceased production. The Tyne Brand factory closed in 1976 and is now a derelict shell. It mirrors the demise of the fishing industry and the herring.

Life inside the Tyne Brand factory.

JIMMY'S STORY

Jimmy Cullen, Chief Engineer, in the centre aboard the *Christania T Purdy*. The skipper in the wheelhouse is Thomas Horsburgh, Geordie Bryson the fireman is to Jimmy's right and on his left is Bobby Parker, 3rd hand.

Jimmy Cullen died in 2001 at the age of 71 years of age and without his help the book may never have been written. At the very least the research period would have been so much longer. He was a walking encyclopaedia on the fishing vessels of North Shields. Little of his knowledge had been committed to paper but stored in filing cabinets in his head. Ask him about any boat and he would tell you where it came from, its North Shields registration, who the skipper and first mate were and invariably the vessel's fate. Such was his knowledge the local library referred people to him when they could not answer their queries. He also had an extensive collection of photographs of fishing vessels, which ran into the thousands. These are currently in my safe keeping.

Jimmy is survived by his son, James Purdy Cullen, who followed his father into the fishing industry and has continued to be of immense help in finalising this book and in checking for factual mistakes.

Jimmy Cullen Snr was the only son of a North Shields family. His father was a fisherman. No other occupation entered his head as a youngster. School for Jimmy was a nuisance, which thwarted his ambitions. In 1941, at the age of thirteen years, Jimmy announced to his mother that he had no intentions of going back to school but that he was going to sea. Such was his resolve that little resistance was met. And so started his love affair with the sea and fishing. Like most affairs, Jimmy was the first to admit that it was a love hate relationship, but one which was difficult to break. A family friend offered him a position as deck hand on a seine net fishing boat at Leith, which he jumped at. A year later he returned to nearer home at Blyth where he worked on another seine net boat. By the age of sixteen, Jimmy was an accomplished fisherman, working at North Shields for William Purdy as one of 'Purdy's Pigs', as local people called them. At seventeen years old he obtained his second engineer's ticket and a year later he became a first engineer, one of the youngest if not the youngest in the area. He finally ceased fishing in 1965.

Jimmy was a quiet man who initially kept his vast information close to his heart until he satisfied himself that the inquirer was not a time waster or someone who was out to exploit his knowledge for their own gain, which unfortunately occurred. However, once you had won his confidence his assistance knew no bounds. His formal education was rudimentary. He spoke from the heart.

The following text is a short story that Jimmy had written. I was privileged to be shown this on one of my many visits. It was dog-eared and grubby but for me it captured his life and inner feelings. I have called it 'Jimmy's Story' because that is what it represents.

I hope you enjoy it.

Jimmy keeping busy in retirement.

Jimmy relaxed in the passenger seat of his old estate car overlooking the mouth of the River Tyne. It was a Sunday afternoon and he had been to the boating lake in Tynemouth Park, sailing his pride and joy, a four-foot scale model of a North Sea steam trawler; a boat built by him with pride. He hadn't used any plans, he didn't need them. Every inch of the model was recreated lovingly from memory. A memory so vivid that he could remember all his time at sea in fishing boats.

Memories of first going through the piers in a steam drifter with his father when he was only seven years old. His pals asking about it the next day.

'What was it like?'

'Were you sea sick?'

'Did you go out of sight of land?'

'Did you sleep? What did you eat? Were you frightened?'

'What did they call the boat?'

And he could recall the pride in his voice when he told them.

'The boat's name's *Achievable*,' he had said.

'She's a Yarmouth drifter, her number is YH 92 and she has got two birds on her funnel.'

The faces of the schoolmates had faded in his mind but he could recall every detail of that first step in his chosen profession. The dash to the school gate, running down the Brewhouse Bank at 4 o'clock on a Friday teatime, past the buildings of the Tyne Brand – 'The Tin Factory' – whose main output those days had been the tinned herrings that were sold worldwide.

His thoughts came back to the present and he thought for a few minutes, about the changes on Brewhouse Bank. The main buildings of the factory were gone. Where they had been was now just a grass-covered slope, the smaller buildings in decay, waiting for their turn to be reduced to rubble, to make way for the planners, whose job it was to change North Shields into some kind of trap for sightseers to come and spend a couple of days thronging along the fish quay.

Artists with paintings for sale hung on nails in the 'The Shed' – the covered part of the fish market that ran along Union Quay Road. All sorts of paintings, the Tyne Piers, the High and Low Lights, St Mary's Island, everything but paintings of the fishermen at sea.

'If only I could write a book,' he thought. 'If only I could tell people what North Shields was all about.'

The years before the war, the times that money was scarce. The look on his mother's face when the wind howled, knowing that her man was out in the storm, somewhere in the North Sea. The weekly trip down 'the stairs' to the trawler owner's office to collect 'the sub'. The sub was an advance of cash to a man's wife whilst he was away at sea. When the boat returned the catch was sold, the wages worked out and the subs deducted, along with money for the food eaten by the crew during the voyage, or the trip as they called it.

Often enough the bad weather or poor fishing resulted in the catch not making enough money to cover the boat's expenses, so there was no share for the crew, who then 'settled in debt'.

YH 82 *Achievable* – the subject of this narrative.

Twenty four hour days! Cold cramped bunks! Wet gear! Sore chapped hands! All for no wages.

'If only I could write a book, I would try to explain all this to the people who buy fish from a shop and who do not even think about where or how it was caught.'

As he watched, a small wooden fishing boat nosed her way into the river around the North Pier. Wondering why she was coming back to the river so soon on a good fishing day he reflected on the changes to fishing in the last thirty years. Gone were the big steamboats, ousted by the bigger diesels that in turn were beaten by increased expenses. Fuel oil prices had rocketed. The cost of repairs, nets and harbour dues had all played their part in the collapse of the deep-sea fleet at North Shields.

The small boat chugging up the river was typical now of the boats of North Shields. About 45 foot long with a crew of three or four.

'She's probably split her nets on a wreck and had to come back to the quay for repairs. Or maybe she's got engine trouble. She's a lot smaller than the *Achievable*,' he muttered to himself as he again remembered that first trip to sea with his father.

The dash down the bank, round the corner at the bottom, past Irvin's office, jumping over wooden fish boxes outside the fish filleting stores. Across the road, through the gate, along the quay, breathless, trembling with the excitement, to where the *Achievable* was lying. Seeing his father standing on the deck. He recalled shouting, 'Dad, help me down the ladder.'

During the school dinner break Jimmy had gone home to see his mother. She had told him his dad would take him to sea if he went straight down when school finished. The skipper had said, 'Yes he could go.' He couldn't remember much about the lessons that day, but he could remember the teacher warning him about looking at the clock so often.

The trip itself was etched on his mind as if it had happened yesterday. *Achievable*, a herring drifter, was a wooden boat, beautifully built; straight stem, and counter stern, well painted and as clean as any boat could be.

On reaching the deck a big pot of hot, sweet tea had been handed to him and he was told to stand beside the wheelhouse. 'Don't get in the way till we are clear of the quay,' he was warned.

Suddenly there was the clang of the bells in the telegraph. The sudden throb of the deck engines were run astern to back away from the wooden beams with the big steel ladders, that had then seemed as high as a house, but were really only about five or six feet above his head.

The telegraph bells jangled again. The engine stopped for a few seconds, and then this time turned the other way forcing the boat ahead. As the propeller pushed her through the water, the bow wave got bigger, and soon white foam was sliding past as they headed down river towards the piers and the open sea.

A voice from the open wheelhouse window above made him look up. The skipper was leaning out of the window, 'Come up here young Jim,' he said. 'Come up in the wheelhouse, then you can't fall over the side.' When he was propped up beside the brass telegraph the skipper said, 'As soon as we get clear of the harbour I'll let you steer.'

Three hours and thirty miles later the boat was stopped and the nets got ready. Then, steaming slowly ahead, the nets were paid out or 'shot' as fishermen term it. Nearly a mile of drift nets, suspended with corks and canvas floats, a heavy footrope on the bottom keeping the nets upright in the water, about ten foot below the surface to catch the herring and the mackerel that swam in shoals and came to the surface in the dark to feed.

His father had the drift watch so he was in the wheelhouse with him. Did he feel tired his father asked?

'No I want to see the nets hauled,' was his eager reply.

As the night wore on talk between them petered out and the quiet of the dark wheelhouse was broken only by the steady creak of the rigging as the drifter slowly rolled on the slight sea.

The slow motion Jimmy felt took its effect and he felt sick. A bucket was placed on the floor beside him; a bucket with rope spliced on the handle just in case he was sick. The rope was tied to the stem of the telegraph. Twice he had tried to make himself sick but he couldn't bring anything up and now he felt as if the whole of the world was spinning. He wished he had stayed at home.

Suddenly the darkness of the night had turned to day. He realised that the whole boat was filled with noise and ablaze with deck lights. He must have dozed off but now the capstan up forward was working. The crew were standing in the well of the deck pulling the nets in with cries of 'spin up my beauties.'

The skipper, watching him wake up asked, 'How are you feeling now?'

The excitement of seeing the men working had for the time being made the sickness not so bad. The nets being pulled over the big wooden roller on the boat's rail didn't look to have many fish in them as they were shook and the fish fell on the deck jumping about like pieces of quicksilver before sliding aft to lie like a glittering silver carpet.

'Very poor,' the skipper moaned.

As the time went by the awful sickness returned. Soon the boat started the run for home to catch the market. He thought he would die after two hours during which time he told everybody, who asked if he was all right, that he would 'Never come to sea again.'

But when the ropes were thrown to the men waiting on the quayside and somebody said, 'I see you've got an extra deckie.' He suddenly felt OK. The tide was just right, and the rail was level with the Quay.

About to jump ashore, he was stopped by one of the crew. 'Wait 'til your dad gets on the Quay first,' he was advised. He waited ten minutes then his father helped him ashore.

What every skipper wants to see – a good haul of fish.

As he took a step he would have fallen but for his father's hand under his arm. 'Just walk and do not look at the ground,' his father said. The funny thing was, the surface of the Quay felt like it was moving, but the feeling soon wore off and so did his resolve to go back to sea.

When August came he was off again back to sea but this time he was on holiday from school and able to spend days on the boat and the sickness was soon a thing of the past.

Now he was not staying in the wheelhouse but helping on the deck and sleeping in his father's bunk down the focsle. At the end of each week taking letters to the post office for the crew who all but for his father came from Yarmouth. Running to the paper shop, getting cigarettes, doing anything that was asked of him brought its reward – a few coppers off each man made him very rich or so it had seemed at the time and he had felt so important. Then the war put him ashore for five years. In August 1939 he had been on a Lowestoft drifter. The last school holidays before the war he was bigger and could do nearly any job at sea but by then he discovered a liking for the engine room, the silver steel rods on the pistons, the cranks, propeller shaft, oil pots, gauges on the boiler and the smell.

He fell in love with the power. He felt happy with a piece of cotton waste in his hand, wiping drops of water off anything that was shiny. The engineer gave him a sweat rag and he wore it proudly around his neck.

Instructions on how to open the fire doors and put coal on the fire bars in the furnaces, how to rake and slice a fire, how to draw a fire – these he learned with enthusiasm.

Even at ten years old, under the watchful eye of the engineer, or driver as they were called in drifters, he could get the ship's engine room ready for sea.

Jimmy's thoughts dwelt for a while on his father. He had been a drifterman for all of his life. He preferred the daily sailings and landings of the herring fishing to the longer trips in the trawlers. In a drifter you didn't make long trips except when changing ports to follow the migrations of the fish shoals.

But he suspected his father enjoyed the time he spent at either Lowestoft or Great Yarmouth. Usually the home fishing for these boats started at the end of September and lasted until Christmas.

But he always returned for Christmas. Always with books, games and chocolates for Jimmy and his younger sister. As the time of the homecoming got near everybody at home waited for the postman's knock; the knock that was accompanied by a letter saying what time he expected to arrive at Newcastle Central Station. His mother would try to take his sister and himself up to meet the train, if it wasn't arriving too late at night.

After the holidays his father would then sign on with one of the local trawler firms until the herring season came around once more. He didn't like it, but it was only for three months until his beloved drifters returned.

This was normally about the beginning of April and it never seemed long before the office of Norford and Suffling, a building situated in the old fort behind the fish market and run by staff from Lowestoft and Yarmouth, sent for him to join a ship. Then he was happy.

But as Jimmy remembered only too well the Government needed the boats that last September to use as minesweepers and at eleven years old he thought his world had come to a sudden stop.

No more boats to sail on. The fish market was taken over by the Navy and surrounded with barbed wire ...

Jimmy never completed this story but I do not think that it detracts from the passion and feelings that he conveys in his very simple and uncomplicated way.

A Fisherman Allergic To Fish!

Bob Cawley at the age of 38 years.

Bob Cawley is now 78 years of age and lives in North Shields with his wife and daughter surrounded by memories of the sea. He is the personification of everyone's picture of 'Salty Sam' but his life could have been so different had fate not taken a hand.

Bob was born in North Shields but did not enjoy a happy childhood. His mother died during the Second World War from injuries sustained during a German air raid and his father had always been abusive and uncaring. Life as a child and a young man was hard and he suffered from rickets due to malnutrition. Breakfast was bread and dripping with generally no lunch. He could have had free school meals but the family would not suffer the 'shame' of claiming the meals so Bob went hungry. Their perceived shame outweighed Bob's hunger. He remembers vividly that on one occasion he was given the top off his father's boiled egg with a piece of bread as his main meal.

In many respects the Second World War came to Bob's rescue. As soon as he was eighteen years old he joined the Royal Navy and commenced his love affair with the sea. Now he had a family, a sense of belonging and he was away from North Shields. Bob was one of the lucky ones and returned home unscathed but back to a home environment that had not changed except that a woman who Bob did not like had replaced his mother. She did not cook or clean but obviously had some attributes that appealed to his father.

Not long after he returned home he had an argument with his father's paramour and made it plain that he thought that she should leave the house. However, it was Bob who was forced to leave.

Bob headed for home that evening following the argument with the woman who was occupying his mother's place fully expecting a confrontation with is father. He was right but there was little confrontation. He had given his father the excuse that he was seeking.

His clothes and belongings were lying on the ground outside his house. Bob was no longer welcome in the family home. His father had finally disowned him and thrown him out. He was devastated. He was penniless, homeless and without a home he was now unemployed. Bob started to aimlessly wander around North Shields. He had nowhere to go and his spirits were low as he sunk further and further into a depression. Life seemed pointless and thoughts of suicide occupied his mind. It seemed the only solution and he decided that he would drown himself by throwing himself into the river. He reasoned that if he changed his mind whilst he was in the water he could always swim to the shore.

Late that night Bob found himself on the Fish Quay by the waters edge looking down into the cold murky waters of the River Tyne. It was a dark miserable night and the Fish Quay was surprisingly quiet. The tide was out and the dark black river glistened like oil way below him. He could make out the shape of the trawlers and drifters tied up along the Fish Quay which all seemed deserted. Bob teetered on the edge trying to summon up the courage to jump when a light came on below him and a friendly voice shouted up in a broad Geordie accent 'Hello there'. It was the ship's night watchman on board a Richard Irvin trawler, the Aberdeen registered *Ocean Fisher*.

'Come on doon, do ye want a cup o' tea,' he shouted as he waved a steaming white pot of tea. Bob needed no further encouragement and was quickly on board. It was good to feel the movement of the boat on the waves. As Bob confided with the night watchman of his plight he drank the strongest, sweetest tea he had ever had. It was good and his spirits started to rise. The night watchman allowed him to stay on board for the night in one of the crew's curtain bunks. He slept well; thoughts of suicide were long gone. He had made up his mind; he wanted to go back to sea.

Early the next morning Bob was awakened by the owner of the boat who wanted to know from the night watchman what a stranger was doing on board his boat. The night watchman explained that Bob was down on his luck. Before Bob could explain his presence on board the owner asked him if he could cook. Seizing the opportunity he quickly replied that he could which he could not. He did not have the first idea on how to cook but he could recognise the opportunity of a job and somewhere to live. A few hours later Bob was signed on as the new cook on board the *Ocean Fisher*.

The *Ocean Fisher* sailed that night but not before Bob had sought out a family friend and had been given a crash cookery course together with a copy of the Bero Cook Book. Bob's first meal was a huge fry up in a frying pan the size of a dustbin lid. This was the traditional meal cooked and eaten before setting sail for the fishing grounds. Sausages, liver, kidneys and chops were all cooked in a lake of hot smoking lard.

Hungry men need feeding.

This meal encouraged the crew to leave the pub in time for the sailing. They tried their best to get Bob drunk in the pub as the boat could not sail without a cook but Bob was made of sterner stuff and managed to get through his first initiation test. The meal was heartily consumed with no complaints and so started Bob's foray into culinary cuisine.

Cooking on board a steam trawler for ten men was not without its difficulties and dangers. The boat rolled and bucked its way to the fishing grounds but the food had to be cooked on time including fresh bread and scones. There was no electric lighting on board; only two carbide lamps lit the galley, one on each side of the stove. Bob soon had a new hairstyle just like he had seen in the comics and books. Bob became a Mohican as he burnt the hair off both sides of his head when he frequently came into contact with the carbide lamps as he tried to cook in the heavy seas.

The *Ocean Fisher* had a good trip trawling for cod, haddock and skate and had one particularly heavy catch whilst she was 165 miles off the coast at Aberdeen, when she brought up in her nets the fuselage of a German Messerschmitt fighter. The pilot had long since departed from the controls but had left his boots behind. The nets were damaged following this incident, which necessitated a visit to Aberdeen to land the remains of the aircraft and repair the nets.

Towards the end of the trip one of the fish landings caught the local trawlermen's favourite dish, a Rock Cod, also known as a Wolf Fish or North Sea Cat, which resembles a catfish. Bob was quickly dispatched to prepare this delicacy for the evening meal. Bob was not used to handling fish and this fish was particularly slimy. The fish was skinned and the catfish stew prepared in a large baking tray. A strong beef stock was made and the chunks of catfish were laid in the stock. A large number of sliced onions were laid over the top of the catfish and the dish stewed for a number of hours. The meal went down well and Bob was feeling at home and one of the crew. However, his newfound luck was to be dealt a cruel blow. Bob's hands began to react to the fish slime but he did not realise how bad the reaction was going to be.

The *Ocean Fisher* returned to North Shields shortly afterwards and then immediately set sail for a three day fishing trip but Bob's days as a trawlerman were, unknown to him, down to single figures. His career was to come to an abrupt halt. The reaction to the fish slime turned into blood poisoning and Bob became very ill. The trawler returned to North Shields and Bob was hospitalised despite the hospital complaining that he smelled of fish! He eventually recovered but his allergic reaction to fish had put paid to his chance of working on the trawlers.

Bob's new career had lasted all of 23 days. What had seemed to be his salvation had nearly cost him his life. However, he had regained his self-esteem and his love of the sea continued as he started a new career as a merchant seaman.

Bob still relives his days as the cook on the *Ocean Fisher*. His wages for the 23-day trip settled at £3 12 shillings and 6 pence (£3 62^1/$_2$p) but he would not have missed the experience for the world.

NO THIRTY-FOOT WAVES ON THE RIVER TYNE

The senseless frenzy of cold green seas.

Adventure for many of the children of today is a trip to Disneyland or the latest video game. Television and DVD has brought everything that much closer and many people would say that our offspring's childhood is the richer for that but there is no substitute for experience at first hand.

Peter Forster was born in 1936 and by the time he was nine years old, just at the end of the Second World War, he was spending all his summer school holidays on board the *Olden Times* (SN 42) where his father Tommy was the cook. Tommy was known as the 'Chip King' for every meal was accompanied by huge helpings of the largest, fattest chips imaginable, all fried in beef dripping. There is no taste like it but sadly health concerns have sounded the end of the greasy chip.

The *Olden Times* was built during the First World War as a Strath Class Admiralty trawler, steam powered and having a gross tonnage of 202 tons. As an admiralty trawler she had carried the pennant number 425 and been named RN *Joshua Budget*. In 1934 she came to North Shields where she remained until she was scrapped in 1950.

The *Olden Times* was typical of her breed. Despite being well worked and rusting she was still a capable sea boat. Tommy and Peter enjoyed two good years on board the *Olden Times* before Tommy moved on to the newer Aberdeen registered but locally owned *Lynne Purdy* (A 60).

These trips were not just day trips, fishing just off the mouth of the Tyne, but ten to fourteen day trips deep into the North Sea in Norwegian and Icelandic waters. When the weather was rough there was no going home or getting off a fantasy ride that was making you feel ill. This was the real world with real excitement tinged with fear.

The *Lynne Purdy* leaving the Tyne on another trip.

By the age of eleven years old Peter had been to the Faroe Islands and watched the islanders whale hunting with the ensuing slaughter after the whales had been corralled and driven ashore. For the Faroe Islanders this was their tradition. It also ensured that they had plenty of whale meat to last them through the dark Arctic winters.

The Faroe Islands sometimes felt like a godforsaken place stuck out in the North Atlantic and it was a source of wonderment to eleven-year-old Peter that people wished to live in such a place. The eighteen inhabited islands lie 270 miles South East of Iceland, 375 miles West of Norway and 190 North West of Scotland. Get into trouble out here and chances of survival and rescue are very slim. The Northern Oceanic climate is cold, wet, miserable, changeable and frequently stormy with temperature all the year round between 3 and 9 degrees Celsius.

SN 265 *Thomas W Irvin* – Peter's first trawler.

By this time Peter was aware that his future lay as a trawlerman and as soon as he reached the age of sixteen years he signed on as an apprentice on the Irvin trawler the *Thomas W Irvin* (SN 265). He was now an accomplished fishermen and quickly progressed up the scale, working wherever the opportunities and the money was the best. Peter favoured fishing in the Icelandic waters and worked the large trawlers out of Hull, Grimsby, Fleetwood and Lowestoft.

In 1960 Peter was back at North Shields and had met the girl who was to become his wife. He was a well-respected fishermen and work was easy to find once you had a good reputation. He now had his mate's ticket and was considering going for his skipper's ticket, which would mean a spell ashore at the Marine College. He signed up for the *Amerique* (SN 92).

Peter Forster at the wheel.

The *Amerique* was a French-built steam trawler, built in 1943 and had originally been named the *Boulonnais*. By now, although she was still powered by steam, she was oil-fired instead of by coal.

The *Amerique* was a graceful looking boat but her looks were deceiving. She always appeared to be sitting low in the water. She had a bad reputation and had lain idle for almost three years in Aberdeen after losing three crewmembers off the Faroe Islands when they had been washed overboard. She had then been bought by Purdy's and transferred to North Shields where many North Shields skippers shunned her.

On 2nd December 1961 the *Amerique* set sail on a 21-day trip for Icelandic waters with Peter as bosun. The skipper was from Hull and was a legend in his own mind. The crew were uneasy and the peculiarities of the *Amerique* quickly started to show themselves.

During the conversion from coal power to oil power a large fuel tank had been installed deep in the hold of the vessel but the tank was not partitioned or honeycombed. This was fine for the first day or two but as this 200 ton tank of heavy crude oil started to be depleted as the vessel headed out on the long trip to Iceland the fuel oil started to wash around in the tank and destabilise the boat. It was almost as if the vessel was top heavy. In the rolling seas the trawler would heel over to port but as it tried to right itself the heavy fuel oil was still moving with the first roll and prevented the vessel from coming upright. Consequently the vessel travelled along at 45 degrees off the horizontal for a considerable period of time and when she eventually righted herself the fuel oil then made a leisurely dash to the starboard side of the tank and sent the boat heeling over the other way at 45 degrees. All the time this was happening the trawler was shipping water across her decks.

Normally this unusual behaviour would be lessened as the holds started to fill up with fish but this trip was a nightmare. Day after day the heavy seas battered the boat and the skipper's assertion that he would fill the holds of the ship in record time started to have a hollow ring.

This trip was the worst that Peter had ever encountered and although he was not frightened of the sea he had a healthy respect for its power and the tenuous grasp that all sailors have on their lives. The weather was getting no better and they were in a senseless frenzy of cold green seas surrounded by 30-foot high waves. Peter decided that he needed to record the seas and struggled forward on the open deck and lashed himself to the forward winch clinging on dearly to his little box Brownie camera. He also tied a strong rope around his waist, which trailed behind him and was held in the safe hands of his friend Geordie Stagg. The agreement was that Peter would try and get one good picture of the sea conditions and then Geordie was to pull with all his might and get Peter off the deck and into the comparative safety of the ship's interior.

As you can see from the picture at the start of this story Peter got his picture and lived to tell the tale.

The *Amerique* returned to North Shields on 23rd December 1961 and landed less than 150 boxes of fish. It was a very poor landing and hardly paid the vessel's way. Peter had had enough and a decision had to be made between going for his skipper's ticket or joining the police

The *Amerique* returning home.

force, which he had been considering for some time.

A friend told him that the River Tyne Police were recruiting. He immediately applied, passed the examination and interview and swapped life on the North Sea for life on the River Tyne without the 30-foot waves as PC 21. But that is another story.

Peter still lives in North Shields with the wife Maureen, the girl he was courting during that eventful trip on board the *Amerique*. The *Amerique* went to the scrapyard in 1967.

It is somewhat ironic that the Purdy family who brought the application of steam to the fishing industry with the conversion of the *Messenger* also brought the very last steam powered boat to North Shields that was such a rogue vessel.

Some light relief on board – 'I see no ships.'

'WHAT WAS THE REASON FOR YOU LEAVING YOUR LAST BOAT?' – 'COS IT WAS SINKING.'

James (Jimmy) Purdy Cullen at sea.

This is the first hand account of the sinking in 1979 of the *Constellation* 110 miles out in the North Sea. Where appropriate Jimmy Cullen's direct words are used in quotation marks.

James Purdy Cullen is 52 years of age and like his father and his grandfather went to sea as a fisherman as soon as he left school. No thought entered his head of any other occupation even though the fishing industry was already showing signs of decline. He had been brought up with the salt water in his veins and like many fishermen he remembered the good times and the good catches when money was good. After all he reasoned – it cannot be all that bad when he recalled his dad owning three Jaguar motor cars in the 1950s and '60s.

Fishing is not just about a job; it is a way of life. Everyone works together and the hard life bonds the community and friendships are made for life. The old adage of a problem shared is a problem solved is true. What is mine is yours if you need it.

In 1979 Jimmy, as he prefers to be called, was skipper on a Lowestoft registered diesel powered trawler called the *Constellation* (LH 245) with a crew of six. The beloved steam trawlers that his father so loved had long gone. The *Constellation* was a wooden hulled motor fishing vessel built at Peterhead. She was a good sea boat, happy in most seas and Jimmy was having a good season fishing out of Eyemouth. The crew was sound although] one of them, Brian Ashley, was a giant of a man who topped the scales at over 23 stone.

Jimmy at work mending nets and gutting fish. No room for idle hands at sea.

Unfortunately during a visit to the Tyne the *Constellation* caught fire when she was moored at the Royal Albert Docks and serious damage was caused to her engine room, the wheelhouse and the deck.

The *Constellation* was repaired at a shipyard on the Tyne and Jimmy received the boat to his command at the beginning of November. The *Constellation* needed some sea trials before she could return to fishing and it was agreed that Jimmy would steam her up to Cockmenzies, near Port Seton, Edinburgh, and back.

The omens from the start were not good. As Jimmy tried to manoeuvre the *Constellation* into the river away from the quay she kept hitting the quay with her bow. 'I thought I was losing my marbles until I figured it out, the daft ******** at the shipyard had fitted the hydraulic steering pump backside forwards.' The effect was that as Jimmy turned to starboard (right) the boat steered to port (left). Jimmy did not want any further delay so he took the boat to sea to check her out. In order to counteract the steering problem Jimmy stood in front of the steering wheel and steered with his hands behind his back.

The problems continued thoughout the trials. The steering problem was corrected at Cockmenzies when the steering pump was turned around but the engine lost oil pressure off Berwick, which necessitated further repairs.

On 28th September 1980 the *Constellation* set sail from the Tyne on a five day fishing trip. Jimmy headed for the Philips oil pumping station number 3656, fifty six miles East North East of the Tyne. Jimmy favoured the area. Two ships, one of which was called the *St Lucia*,

Fishing in good weather.

A companion at sea landing its catch.

guarded the pumping station. Jimmy knew the captain and crew well and was assured of a warm welcome.

The trip was going fine and Jimmy felt good to be back at sea with a good crew and a good boat. The weather was typical November. Grey, miserable with stroppy, lumpy seas. After exchanging pleasantries with the *St Lucia*, Jimmy pointed the *Constellation* further out into the North Sea looking for that good catch.

The *Constellation* was 110 miles off North Shields on the last day of fishing when one of the crew told Jimmy that the engine room was full of water. Jimmy's heart dropped like a stone as he peered into the engine room and saw seawater lapping around the engine cradle. He climbed down into the cold oily water hoping to find the problem. He found the problem all right. The bilge pumps weren't working. They were blocked with wood shavings from the shipyard repairs. Instead of pumping water out, the pumps were allowing water in. They were in serious trouble and the safety of the crew was in Jimmy's hands. 'It's funny at this point I was not too concerned. I thought we could fix the problem.'

Jimmy started the auxiliary motor that was mounted above the main engine, which would at least give them some independent electrical power. 'I got a message off to the *St Lucia* telling them that we were taking in water and asked them to put out a non-emergency call of all shipping and to monitor us on Channel 16.'

At this point the engine failed and the boat lost all power. The situation was now becoming critical. 'I shouted up the *St Lucia* again and asked them to put out a mayday on our behalf. I also asked them for their assistance.'

The *Constellation* was now at the mercy of the seas and good fortune. Jimmy had no idea how quickly she was taking in water and the nearest help was at least 50 miles away. He decided to prepare to abandon ship and readied the crew to launch the inflatable life raft. The life raft was readied, a line attached from it to the *Constellation* and the life raft launched. Brian was told to get aboard and 23 stone of unbridled flesh fell from the *Constellation* into the life raft. There was an enormous explosion as Brian hit the life raft, the thing folded in two and a rush of air bubbles rushed to the surface. '**** me I thought, he's gone straight through the bloody raft.'

Fortunately Brian had not burst the raft but had released the trapped air beneath the life raft as he had performed his Olga Korbitt trampoline act. The crew quickly boarded the life raft but there was no room for Jimmy. A 23 stone man takes up at least two places. Well they say that the skipper always goes down with his ship but Jimmy was not too convinced of the sense of the argument at this moment in time.

Jimmy remained on board the *Constellation* but she was settling deeper and deeper into the water. She was a lost cause and was in her death throes. 'I was starting to get a little concerned, no to be honest I was getting panicky when the *St Lucia* appeared on the horizon. She may not have been the prettiest ship I had seen but at this time she was Marilyn Monroe, Sabrina and Diana Dors all wrapped up together.'

The skipper of the *St Lucia* was a superb seaman and ran his boat alongside the *Constellation*, which was no main feat. On the rise of a wave Jimmy jumped aboard and the rest of the crew were quickly on board and warmly ensconced below decks.

The *St Lucia* managed to get a towline on to the *Constellation* and set course for North Shields with Jimmy alongside the captain. It looked as if there was a chance to save the boat. No one wants to lose a boat especially when it had 70 boxes of fish on board.

For eight hours the *St Lucia* towed the *Constellation* towards North Shields. The speed of the tow managed to keep the head of the boat up and hopes were high that she would be saved. However, it was not to be. 'We were doing well but the weather worsened and the *St Lucia* had to slow down. The bow of the *Constellation* settled in the water and then I heard a sound like I have never heard before. I do not want to hear it again. A large amount of water had settled in the stern but as the head dropped this water came rushing forward. One by one I heard the internal bulkheads smash and give way. The *Constellation* slowly rolled over on to her side and went straight down. I had to look away as she disappeared below the water.' The *Constellation* sank at 6.30 am on Saturday, 4th October 1980.

The *St Lucia* landed Jimmy and his crew later that Saturday at North Shields, seven days after she had left the Tyne on such high hopes. After a quick thank you, the *St Lucia* left to return to her guard station at the Philips oil pumping station. Jimmy now had to deal with a Board of Trade and Insurance investigation. He was exonerated of all blame.

On the following Monday, Jimmy and the crew presented themselves at the 'North Shields Dole Office.' As fishermen they were allowed to sign on in bad weather or during a period of ship repairs or idleness. The clerk started to warily fill out the necessary forms asking the same questions in that monotone voice that they seem to develop. 'And the reason for leaving your last boat Mr Cullen?' she asked.

Jimmy stoically replied with a dead pan expression, 'Cos she was sinking.' His claim was allowed and immediately backdated. The three-day lying on period was backdated to the time of the sinking. Who says that civil servants have no compassion?

Jimmy ceased to be a fisherman in 1986.

Jimmy's father, James Cullen, wrote a letter of appreciation on behalf of his son, to the crew of the *St Lucia* but for reasons best known to him it was never posted. It may not be the most eloquent of letters but that does not detract from the high regard that the skipper and the crew of the *St Lucia* are held in. The letter is reproduced below and if you were a member of the crew of the *St Lucia* – thank you.

Dear Skipper,

I would like you and your crew to accept the crew's and my sincere thanks for the able and most invaluable assistance and the promptness of the action that was given to us on the sinking of my ship the 'Constellation' and the substantial effort which you all put in in the attempt to reach port with my ship.

Once again very many thanks indeed to you and your 'lads' for a job well done.

Yours sincerely
James Purdy Cullen.

Jimmy Cullen Jr today with his loyal friend Domino.

THE MYSTERIOUS
LOSS OF THE
JEANIE STEWART

The SN 18 *Jeanie Stewart*.

Iris Brunton was just eleven years old when her father Ralph failed to return home following the loss of the *Jeanie Stewart*. Sixty four years later she still grieves for a father she loved and to this day the tragic circumstances surrounding the loss of SN 18 *Jeanie Stewart* with all hands remains a mystery.

Annie, the wife of Ralph Brunton.

Iris was born on the Fish Quay where she lived with her parents and one brother and sister. Her grandparents lived near by in this close-knit community and she rarely ventured forth away from the Quay. Money has always tight but she never felt poor and besides she had the Fish Quay as her playground.

Iris and her friends would paddle in the dirty waters of the Fish Quay sands without a moment's thought for the pollution and would wander around the Quay watching the fish being gutted, the boats and the men who worked them. The mortuary was situated on the Fish

Iris' playground – herring drifters tied up at the Fish Quay.

Quay – 'the dead house' – and she and her friends would frighten themselves by looking though a hole in the door to see if anyone was in temporary residence.

She felt very close to her community and lived a happy childhood, certainly up until she lost her father.

The *Jeanie Stewart* was a steel steam trawler, which was built in Aberdeen in 1916 with a gross tonnage of 210 tons. She was originally registered at Hull as H 82 but by 1920 she had become part of the Richard Irvin fleet and had been registered at North Shields as SN 18. She was a proud little ship and served during the First World War as a minesweeper returning to fishing duties in 1919.

On 10th December 1938 the *Jeanie Stewart* headed over the harbour bar at Tynemouth for the fishing grounds in the North Sea off the Norwegian coast with a complement of seven North Shields and two other crewmembers. She was carrying sufficient food provisions for a fourteen-day trip and sufficient coal for eighteen days.

Her skipper was a well known and respected local trawler man called Fred Mills and the crew was made of as follows:

> Frederick Mills, Skipper, Highbury Place, North Shields
> A. Rowe, Chief Engineer, Princess Street, North Shields
> T. Dockey, Second Engineer, Chirton Green, North Shields
> S. Cottingham, Fireman, West Percy Road, North Shields
> A.E. Stockton, Deck Hand, Whitby Street, North Shields
> R. Brunton, Third Hand, Percy Square, North Shields
> H. Maltby, Upper Penman Street, North Shields
> J.B. Grewcock, Edith Street, South Shields
> W.G. Hopkins, Mate, Grays Square, Hartlepool

The *Jeanie Stewart* was expected to be back in port in time for the Christmas market as was the tradition of this skipper. The trawler in common with all trawlers of that time carried a radio which could only receive messages so once she was at sea she was at the mercy of the elements and the skill of her crew.

On 24th December 1938 another Irvin trawler, A40 *Ben Chourn,* saw the *Jeanie Stewart* approximately 50 miles off the mouth of the River Tyne. A force eight gale was blowing and the sea was running a six metre swell. Visibility was quite poor and the *Jeanie Stewart* was lost from view as darkness descended. This was the last sighting of the *Jeanie Stewart* and nothing has been found of her or her crew since.

As Christmas Day approached and there continued to be no sign of the *Jeanie Stewart*, fears started to grow for their safety. Wives, children and family members tried to console themselves with the thought that perhaps the vessel was struggling home with some form of engine problem, was lying disabled with engine failure or was sheltering out the storm. Many of them kept a vigil at vantage points overlooking the harbour entrance but to no avail.

On 27th December 1938 a steam trawler was seen and heard heading for the Tyne blasting its steam whistle. Scores of people on both sides of the river rushed out of their houses braving the driving rain under the assumption that the *Jeanie Stewart* had made it home. Eyes strained through the gloom to identify the trawler. It was not long before the anticipated joy turned to disappointment. The steam trawler was not the *Jeanie Stewart* and the reason for the noise was a jammed steam whistle.

A number of SOS messages were radioed out to trawlers seeking their assistance in finding the *Jeanie Stewart* but without success. The *Jeanie Stewart* had just vanished.

On 2nd January 1939 the Aberdeen fishing trawler *Horace E Nutten* picked up a makeshift raft 90 miles off the coast at Aberdeen. The raft was made up of fish boxes nailed together and lashed together with rope. A barrel had been lashed to one corner to aid buoyancy and this barrel bore the letters RI and NS. All Irvin trawlers carried the same type of barrels to hold the cod livers taken from the fishing during gutting at sea and it was widely thought that the barrel was from Richard Irvin's of North Shields hence the initial RI and NS. Had the *Jeanie Stewart* suffered a catastrophe, which had sunk her but which had allowed the crew time to construct a life raft, or was this a cruel irony of fate. Had a raft once constructed by the children on the North Shields Fish Quay floated out to sea and due to the prevailing tides and currents been carried to Aberdeen where it was found by the *Horace E Nutten*. No one will ever know.

The Ministry of Agriculture and Fisheries, however, reached the decision with the discovery of the life raft that this was conclusive evidence that the *Jeanie Stewart* had foundered and been lost.

The seven North Shields men were all married and had families. The Borough Treasurer set up a relief fund for the families and the first

The use of the North Shields to South Shields Ferry by Iris was a great adventure.

donation was reputedly £100 from Richard Irvin, the trawler owner.

In all over twenty dependants were left without any means of support following the deaths of their husbands and fathers.

Mr A.E. Stockton, who was named as a resident of North Shields, had only just moved into the area from Great Yarmouth and his wife is reported in the local newspapers to have said, 'My husband came up from Yarmouth to join the North Shields fishing fleet and we have had no opportunity of saving any money. My relations cannot possibly provide for us and the relief fund will help us to live while I decide what is to be done.'

The mother of Iris Brunton is also quoted as having said, 'If he is not safe by then (New Year's Eve) I will know something has happened but in the meantime I can only hope and pray that she has taken shelter somewhere and cannot get word through.' Unfortunately her prayers were not answered.

The *Jeanie Stewart* is only one of many North Shields trawlers to be lost with all hands but this story shows the effect that these losses had upon whole communities. The sea is a hostile element with no conscience. The price of fish can never to be too high. Its costs should be measured in human lives and tragedy as well as what it costs in money.

Spare a thought for Iris the last surviving member of Ralph Brunton's family. Iris has no grave to visit to pay her respects. She is still haunted by her father's untimely death in that unknown grave they call the sea.

In Waters Shallow

In waters shallow, in waters deep,
in your hands O'Lord their safety keep.
For the boats which go out lining,
bring them home, so there's no pining.

In boats large or in boats small,
they all suffer from the sudden squall.
With rain lashed faces, body and hands,
each about their task they bravely stand.

With winds that come with sudden force
from the east, south, west and north.
With raging seas that test man and boat to their limit,
this sea from flat calm to a gale in just a minute.

Where sand banks run and great seas boil,
this is the place where loved ones sweat and toil.
The fish we eat at what great cost,
this harvest is paid for with lives lost.

The families who sit at home
and listen to the wild winds moan,
Their prayers O'Lord please hear my plea,
because my dad sails on your sea.

The sun now shines in all its glory,
this time no sad end to this story.
Because Lord you've heard my plea,
my dad's boat is home safely tied against the quay.

Nicola Webb (aged 13) 1997
Published by courtesy of the *Fishing News*

TRAWLERS IN THE WARS

Armed trawler HMT *Lilac* on patrol during the Second World War.

Commercial fishing was a dangerous occupation in peacetime but the greatest losses were inflicted during both world wars and in particular during the Great War. Vast numbers of fishing vessels were requisitioned during both wars and many were built during the First World War for Royal Naval Patrol Service. At the same time many remained in service for commercial fishing when they had to endure the additional dangers from mines, attacks from enemy aircraft and submarines alongside the dangers of the sea.

At the onset of the First World War all fishing vessels were ordered back to port. This was not an easy task as very few had wireless. In excess of 85% of all fish caught was landed at the fishing ports bordering the North Sea and it was not long before many of the trawlers returned to sea to resume fishing despite the additional dangers. They paid a heavy price.

By 1914 the number of trawlers registered at North Shields exceeded 118 but this fleet was rapidly depleted following the outbreak of the First World War. The Government requisitioned large numbers of vessels for duties with the Royal Navy. These vessels were a rough and ready fleet of coal burning trawlers, drifters and whalers which were hurriedly given single 6 pounder and 12 pounder guns, minesweeping gear and asdic sounding equipment and sent off to war as minesweepers, convoy escorts, U boat hunters and auxiliary patrol vessels.

The vessels were invariably crewed by fishermen and their officers were skippers from the fishing fleets with an input from the Royal Navy

SN 275 *Lily* – one of the first mercantile casualties of the First World War.

and the Royal Naval Reserve in an attempt to instil formal discipline. However, the fishermen's stubborn independence and casual approach to discipline belied their special brand of bloody mindedness, determination and sheer guts. 'Harry Tate's Navy,' they may have been called in the Second World War, after the famous comedian who had difficulty with all things mechanical, but these little ships and their crews are remembered with pride and they won the admiration of their comrades in the bigger ships.

Trawlers and drifters used to the North Sea found themselves in the Atlantic, off the eastern seaboard of America, Gibraltar and the Mediterranean, Africa, India and the Far East travelling journeys of thousands of miles.

During the course of the First World War, thirty five North Shields trawlers were recorded as lost on active service and whilst engaged on commercial fishing.

Mercantile Losses

The first vessel lost was SN 275 *Lily*. On 8th October 1914 she struck a mine twenty eight miles East by North of the River Tyne. Five members of her crew were killed.

SN 254 *Nellie* became a casualty of war when a German submarine captured her on 1st April 1915, thirty five miles North East by East of the River Tyne. A bomb was placed on board and the vessel sunk.

On 28th April 1915 SN 38 *Lilydale* was fishing thirty seven miles east of St Abbs Head when a German submarine captured her. A bomb was placed on board and detonated which sunk the vessel. It is not known if any members of the crew perished.

SN 49 *St George* was captured less than one month later on 2nd May 1915 by a submarine, sixty five miles East of Aberdeen. The crew were made prisoners of war and the vessel sunk by gunfire. The same day a submarine sixty five miles East by North of May Island captured SN 101 *St Louise No 1*. She was sunk by gunfire.

On 24th July 1915 SN 251 *Anglia* was captured by a German submarine thirty five miles North West by West of Sunlisker and sunk by gunfire. No details have been found of any casualties.

SN 58 *Saxon Prince* served as minesweeper No 262 between August 1914 and March 1916 without a scratch and returned to fishing duties. On 28th March 1916 the trawler disappeared in a storm off Dover with the loss of nine lives. Tynemouth Roll of Honour shows the following people as lost.

> G.O. Smails, Coburg Street, North Shields
> T. Tomlinson, Bell Street, North Shields
> T.R. Tomlinson, Bell Street, North Shields
> R. Charters, Stephenson Street, North Shields
> C.M. Proffit, Linskill Street, North Shields
> T. Lorimer, Pant Street, North Shields
> G.A. Rose Tyne Street, North Shields

Between 5th and 6th July 1916 three North Shields registered vessels, SN 154 *Nancy Hunnam*, SN 229 *Newark Castle* and SN 299 *Annie Anderson,* together with four Scottish and South Country boats were captured and sunk by enemy submarines off the Northumberland coast. The *Annie Andersen* was a sailing lugger fitted with an auxiliary motor but was obviously considered to be fair game.

On 14th July 1916 SN 89 *Langley Castle* and SN 293 *Recorder* met their end at the hands of a German submarine eighteen miles North East by East of the River Tyne. Bombs were detonated on board and the vessel sunk.

A rare photograph of SN 293 *Recorder*.

On 28th July 1916 seven drifters, none registered at North Shields, were sunk by submarines fourteen miles North East of the River Tyne. Only days later in a four-day period between 2nd August and 5th August 1916 seven trawlers were sent to a watery grave off the mouth of the River Tyne by German submarines. Six of these trawlers were from North Shields namely SN 3 *Egyptian Prince*, SN 21 *St Olive*, SN 108 *Lucania*, SN 241 *Trawler Prince*, SN 253 *Merchant Prince* and SN 258 *Rhodesia*.

Fishermen are by nature superstitious and it would not be surprising if they believed that any fishing boat bearing the name 'Prince' at the

end of its name would bring bad luck. In all 32 boats named *******
Prince were North Shields registered and seventeen of them were lost at
sea or through enemy action.

SN 174 *Viella* became another mercantile casualty on 23rd
September 1916 when the vessel was captured by a submarine thirty
eight miles South East from Spurn Light Vessel. A bomb was placed on
board and the vessel sunk.

In January 1917 SN 239 *Agnes* was captured by an enemy submarine
in the North Sea and sunk by unknown means. Her crew of nine,
despite being engaged on mercantile duties were made prisoners of
war.

SN 328 *Excel* had been only at the port of North Shields for one
month before she became a casualty of war. A submarine captured her
on 17th February 1917, fifty three miles North East of the River Tyne.
The vessel was sunk by gunfire and there is no record of any casualties.

Between 22nd and 28th January 1917 SN 324 *George E Benson* was
sunk or captured by an enemy submarine somewhere in the North Sea.
The crew of nine were made prisoners of war.

On 17th May 1917 SN 48 *Dilston Castle* was sent to the bottom of the
ocean by a submarine sixteen miles East of Aberdeen. A bomb was
placed on board and detonated sinking the vessel.

SN 111 *John M Smart* was captured by an enemy submarine on 12th
December 1917, ten miles East of the River Tyne. She was sunk by
gunfire with the loss of four lives. The Tynemouth Roll of Honour
details the following fatalities.

> G.O. Mudale, Chief Engineer
> W.J. Kenny, Pant Street, North Shields

On the same day SN 300 *Ranter* was heavily shelled by a German
submarine. Four crewmembers lost their lives. The following fatalities
are officially recorded.

> J.W. Taylor, Dockwray Square, North Shields
> J.R. Weddell, Upper Queen Street, North Shields
> R. Newson, 61 years, no further details
> R. Walkington, no further details

On 27th August 1924 SN 300 *Ranter* was totally lost whilst carrying
a crew of eight. No further details are available.

SN 2 *Reaper* was lost on 21st February 1918, two miles North East of
the River Tyne when she struck a mine. All eight members of the crew
were lost including.

> Alex Hastie, Skipper.
> H. Blackburn, Rudyerd Street, North Shields

On 26th February 1918 SN 247 *Rambler* struck a mine four miles
East of Blyth. The total crew of nine were killed.

Despite the cessation of hostilities the war continued to claim lives
due to the number of unexploded mines in the North Sea. On 1st
December 1918 SN 255 *TW Mould* was lost with all hands thirty miles

North East of the River Tyne after hitting mines. Eight local men lost their lives along with two others from outside the area. The vessel was lost at the same time as SN 344 *Ethelwulf*. The *Ethelwulf* accompanied by SN 248 *Lanercost* left North Shields on 30th November 1918 and joined the fishing fleet, which included the *TW Mould*. The fleet was trawling East North East of the River Tyne when at 3 am on 1st December 1918 two loud explosions were heard in quick succession. Once order was established it was discovered that the *Ethelwulf* and the *TW Mould* had vanished. No bodies were recovered from the sea.

The following fatalities occurred on the *TW Mould*.

> H. Williamson, Skipper, Washington Terrace, North Shields
> A. Wales, Mate, Princess Street, North Shields
> J.T. Kennedy, Chief Engineer, Coburg Street, North Shields
> J.H. Davidson, Second Engineer, Baines Terrace, Sunderland
> G. Crutwell, Third Hand, Robertson Street, South Shields
> R. Angus, Fireman, Church Street, North Shields
> G. Marlborough, Deck Hand, Mellish Road, Poplar
> C.E. Pratt, Deck Hand, Thurbeck Quarters, Boston
> J. Lucas, Cook, Church Street, North Shields
> J. Collins, Gunner, Royal Naval Reserve, Eyemouth

The following fatalities occurred on the *Ethelwulf*.

> R. Steadman, Skipper, Dockwray Square, North Shields
> J. Dodds, Mate (son-in-law of the skipper), Dockwray Square, North Shields
> A. Kinnear, Third Hand, North Shields
> J.J. Jameson, Chief Engineer, Church Street, North Shields
> A. Wray, Deck Hand, North Shields
> A. Smith, Whitley Bay
> J. Grieves, Fireman, South Shields
> E.F. Sankey, Wireless Operator, Royal Naval Reserve, Nottingham

The last mercantile casualty was SN 4 *Grecian Prince*. According to Custom Records she was lost on 17th December 1918 after striking a mine.

Vessels lost on Active Service

In August 1914 SN 202 *Princess Beatrice* was requisitioned as minesweeper No 287. On 5th October 1914 the vessel hit a mine off the Belgian coast and was lost. There is no record of any fatalities.
SN 76 *Jason* was requisitioned as minesweeper No 10 in August 1914.

On 1st April 1915 a submarine captured the vessel when she was 40 miles North East by East of the River Tyne. A bomb was placed on board and the vessel sunk.

In January 1915 SN 184 *Lottie Leask* was requisitioned and served as a net layer No 1072. On 18th December 1915 whilst on active service the vessel was sunk by a submarine off Sasemo Island.

SN 109 *Coral Isle* alongside the ill-fated battleship HMS *Hood*. The *Hood* – one of the Navy's greatest battleships – was later sunk by the *Bismarck*.

SN 312 *Ben Earn* on patrol as HMT *Ben Earn*.

SN 99 *Ben Torc* on naval patrol.

SN 324 *Princess Olga* commenced her duties as minesweeper No 3031 late into the war. On 14th June 1918 she was sunk after striking mines off the coat at Le Havre, France.

Whilst their naval activities were primarily confined to the North Sea on 7th August 1916 SN 233 *John High* sank after striking a mine off Mount Sozonava in the White Sea. The Tynemouth Roll of Honour details the following fatalities.

> R. Newson, Chief Engineer of Howdon, Wallsend
> J. High, St John's Terrace, Percy Main

On 28th March 1918 SN 15 *Princess Alice* was lost off Alexandria, Egypt, following a collision.

Naval construction during the First World War was minimal until 1916, wholesale requisitioning having met naval commitments. However, by this time losses had been high and any further requisitioning would have seriously affected the supply of fish to the population. A massive rebuilding programme was ordered and approximately four hundred trawlers and drifters ordered.

Three classes of trawlers were ordered which accorded with mercantile prototypes designed by individual shipyards. They comprised of the Mersey class, Castle class from Smith's Dock of North Shields and the Strath class from Hall Russells of Aberdeen. In total over 110 Mersey, 197 Castle and 149 Strath class trawlers were ordered. Each was named after a crewmember of HMS *Victory* and HMS *Royal Sovereign* at the time of the Battle of Trafalgar. The normal wartime complement of crew was between fifteen and eighteen men. The average cost per vessel for hull and machinery was £18,000 for a Strath class, £21,000 for a Castle class and £22,000 for a Mersey class.

Upon the cessation of hostilities in November 1918 the government began to release vessels from requisition and return them to their owners. Returning them to commercial service was no simple matter for in most cases several months refitment was required before fishing could be resumed. A large number of Admiralty-built trawlers and drifters returned to the commercial market and despite the glut of trawlers they realised good money, generally half the cost of building them.

The Strath class type of trawler were favoured by the North Shields owners with only one Castle class trawler SN 14 *Lowdock* and one Mersey class trawler SN 109 *Coral Isle* to bear North Shields registrations.

At the onset of the Second World War only fourteen Mersey class, three Castle class and a solitary Strath class trawler remained in Naval Service. Once again substantial requisitioning augmented the Royal Navy. Two hundred and thirty former Mersey, Strath and Castle class trawlers reverted to the Royal Navy. A modest building programme of new and larger types of trawlers supplemented this. Most Naval, including requisitioned trawlers, were armed with four inch guns for anti-submarine work, twelve pounder guns for minesweepers duties,

20 mm anti-aircraft guns, some vintage three and six pounder guns, asdic equipment and depth charges. Fortunately the attrition rate was much less for the North Shields trawlers and drifters this time.

SN 62 *Evelina* was originally built as a Strath class Admiralty trawler No 4203 *John Howard*. On 11th November 1939 the vessel was requisitioned and placed on auxiliary patrol duties. On 14th December 1939 the vessel went missing with a crew of nine men. It is believed to have been lost off the River Tyne probably by hitting a mine. It is believed that a wreck ½ mile East of Souter Lighthouse is the *Evelina*.

SN 62 *Evelina* tied up at North Shields Fish Quay in happy times.

On 9th February 1940 whilst fishing three miles east of Scarborough, SN 14 *Lowdock*, formerly the *Peter Lovett,* was attacked by enemy aircraft. She survived the attacked but only weeks later on 19th March 1940 she was sunk following a collision.

SN 200 *Princess Royal* was an ageing trawler engaged on fishing duties when she was attacked by enemy aircraft on 28th March 1940, forty miles South South West of Bresay Light, Shetland. She lived to tell the tale.

SN 110 *Ben Glamair* was registered at North Shields in 1914 and between May 1915 and 1919 the vessel served as minesweeper No 1494. On 17th July 1941 the vessel went missing after leaving Embelton Bay off the coast of North Northumberland. The crew of ten lost their lives.

SN 14 *Lowdock* shepherding a great liner out of the Tyne

On 8th November 1941 SN 8 *Craddock* was attacked and sunk by enemy aircraft whilst fishing fourteen miles North North East of St Abbs Head. Any loss of life to the crew is unknown.

Less than one month later enemy aircraft attacked SN 217 *St Leonard* No 1 on 1st December 1941 at a position 60 degrees 58 minutes North by 1 degree 10 minutes West. She did not survive the attack and was sunk. It is not known what happened to the crew.

On 2nd June 1941 SN 78 *Ben Screel* survived an attack by enemy aircraft with bombs at position 55 degrees 30 minutes North, 1 degree 30 minutes West. On 12th November 1941 the vessel survived a further attack by enemy aircraft with bombs 14 miles North East by North of St Abbs Head. Eventually luck for this vessel ran out. On 25th December 1942 the vessel was lost off St Abbs Head. It is believed that she hit a mine. Loss of life is unknown. Some Christmas box!.

On patrol during the Second
World War – always vigilant,
despite the weather.

A South African whaler owned
by Irvin and Johnston on Naval
Patrol.

THE A TO Z OF NORTH SHIELDS REGISTERED FISHING VESSELS 1875-1967

SN 133 *John Bennett* at her naming ceremony.

Records and Their Interpretations

Since 1868 fishing boats used for commercial fishing have had to be registered with the Customs and Excise who issued each vessel with a unique identification mark. This consisted of a port designation letter followed by a number. This appears fairly simplistic until it is appreciated that there are three classes of vessel – 1st, 2nd and 3rd.

The regulations defined the vessels as follows:

1st Class includes all steamers and other boats of 15 tons gross tonnage and upwards.

2nd Class includes all steamers and other boats of less than 15 tons gross tonnage, or of 18 feet keel and upwards.

3rd Class includes all boats under 18 feet keel other than those navigated by oars only and marked in accordance with Section 176 of the Customs Consolidation Act 1876.

This book catalogues only 1st class vessels both sailing and steamers between 1875 and 1967. The register runs for 15 years after which vessels that have been de-registered during this period had that number

The *Noogana* arrives in the Tyne in 1935 prior to registration as SN 47 *St Olive*.

reissued. Since 1927 every registered fishing vessel in this category had to have her name and port of registry painted in white oil colour on a black background on the vessel's stern. In the case of steamers, the port of designation and number is painted on each bow and her funnel.

Ist class vessels are generally referred to as trawlers but this has no simple or single meaning. This catalogue, although primarily concerned with steam powered vessels, also includes sail powered luggers and sail powered vessels fitted with auxiliary motors. Once steam gained supremacy the vessels, however, were not automatically classed as trawlers. They are described in early registers as steam powered smacks, ketches, sloops, dandies and yawls but the common denominator is that they worked the North Sea grounds for fish.

During the period researched 542 vessels were North Shields registered which amounted to 505 individual boats (some were registered on more than one occasion). Out of this figure over 27% of these vessels failed to return to port and were lost.

The port designation is generally the first and last letters of that port. Hence the port of Grimsby is GY, Brixham BM and Fleetwood FD. So far so good. However, Hull is not HL but H because Hartlepool as a fishing port registered before them. Aberdeen is not AN but A for some obscure reason despite the fact that AN has never been allocated and Oban is OB and not ON. So can we assume that North Shields is NS? No it is SN because decades ago NS was issued to North Sunderland in Northumberland, which is now more generally known as Seahouses.

The port registration SN, until the beginning of this century, included fishing boats fishing out of Blyth and Newbiggin as well as North Shields vessels. The Newbiggin boats were all sailing luggers and I have found no record of any steam trawlers using Newbiggin as a base whilst carrying the SN port designation.

Port Registrations seen at North Shields

A	Aberdeen	KY	Kirkcaldy
AA	Alloa	LH	Leith
AD	Ardrossan	LK	Lerwick
AH	Arbroath	LT	Lowestoft
AR	Ayr	MH	Middlesbrough
BCK	Buckie	NE	Newcastle
BH	Blyth	OB	Oban
BK	Berwick	PD	Peterhead
DE	Dundee	SD	Sunderland
DS	Dumfries	SH	Scarborough
FD	Fleetwood	SN	North Shields
FR	Fraserburgh	SSS	South Shields
GN	Granton	ST	Stockton
GY	Grimsby	WA	Whitehaven
H	Hull	WK	Wick
HL	Hartlepool	WY	Whitby
INS	Inverness	YH	Great Yarmouth

The North Shields registry of 1st Class vessels commenced at the number SN 944 and I have been unable to find an explanation for this oddity. The register was not rationalised to commence at SN 1 until the year of 1887. The catalogue for simplicity is in alphabetical order.

I, like many people, believed that a complete list of North Shields trawlers and their fate was bound to exist but this was found not to be the case. It may well have existed in some form and in some dusty attic of a Mutual Assurance office but these historically valuable documents were more than likely dumped or destroyed when such institutions were liquidated following the collapse of the fishing industry. The foundation for the catalogue of North Shields fishing vessels rests with the Custom and Excise records of registered fishing vessels and information gleaned from *Olsens Fisherman's Nautical Almanac*, which has been published yearly since 1877. Cataloguing the entire fleet has not been a without its difficulties. Discovering the fate of each and every vessel has been challenge but a very rewarding experience, which has necessitated extensive research from a variety of sources, too many to list.

The Customs and Excise records proved to be an invaluable source of information but it is a register of shipping, not of crews. In the case of trawler losses the registers say little, if anything, about the trawler men, how many lives were lost or how many were rescued or the location of the loss. A number of terms are used in the registers, which are defined as follows.

SANK/FOUNDERED. This category encompasses the terms used in the Victorian registers of foundered at sea. In essence it means a vessel, filled with water and sank during a sudden squall, through storm force seas, high winds, freak waves or other tragedy. Twenty five vessels are recorded as foundered and four as sank.

WRECKED. This means the vessel ran ashore accidentally in fog, through poor navigation or was forced ashore during violent weather. Sixteen vessels are recorded as wrecked.

STRANDED. A stranded trawler is one, which has run ashore and becomes absolutely trapped. More often than not most got off free on the next tide, perhaps with the pull of another ship such as the case of SN 171 *Polar Prince*, which ran aground on 23rd August 1938 in dense fog south of St Mary's Island, Whitley Bay. She was refloated with the aid of the Cullercoats lifeboat *Richard Silver Oliver*. Strandings were not uncommon in the trawling world and the clerks who completed the earlier registers used the term 'stranded' and 'wrecked' in the same context. Five vessels were stranded and became total losses. The most dramatic which was recorded was SN 121 *Rightway* which in November 1932, within a year of building, stranded and was wrecked at Collieston, Scotland. At the time the *Rightway* was the most modern trawler fishing out of North Shields. She lies near the wrecks of SN 71 *William Ferrins* and the Hull registered *City of Osaka*.

The stranding of SN 121 *Rightway* off the coast of Collieston, Scotland, in 1933.

COLLISION. This term is less ambiguous and means a collision between two vessels, which strike each other and as a result one or both sink. The 'run down' category is similar to a collision and undoubtedly refers to a smaller vessel being hit by a larger vessel coming head or side on at speed, the vessel being sunk as a result of the collision. Ten vessels are recorded as lost following a collision.

MISSING OR LOST. Two other 'catch all' categories by the Customs clerks are the missing and lost ones. Missing is often the reason given in the days before wireless was standard trawler equipment. These are very much mystery losses and it is likely that no crewmen survived to tell the tale. *Laytons Nautical Dictionary* describes missing as 'said of a vessel when no news has been heard of her and it is feared but not proved that she has been lost.'

The same air of mystery also surrounds those losses merely labelled as lost. Again I can only refer to the Custom records except where alternative information was acquired from some other reliable source. It may well have been the case that the Customs clerk was aware of the circumstances and details surrounding the loss but for the sake of expediency or brevity they purely recorded loss in the register. Thirty five North Shields vessels succumbed.

CONFLICT. This category is comprehensively detailed in a separate chapter and covers the untimely fate of a trawler during the two world wars as a result of hostile acts. The North Shields Customs registers do not use a specific heading such as conflict but tend to refer to the specific act, which caused the loss. Forty one vessels were sent to the bottom of the sea during both world wars.

As already indicated my primary sources of information relate to trawlers registered at North Shields. These were invariably crewed by local men but like any principle there are exceptions to any rule. A small number of trawlers fished out of North Shields whilst being registered at other ports.

Conversely just because a vessel was registered at North Shields this did not automatically mean that she sailed from that port. However, as a general rule most trawlers registered at North Shields did use the port as their home base. To extend the scope of this book to follow the fortunes of North Shields trawlers registered elsewhere or to try to document the fate of trawlers registered elsewhere but using North Shields as their homeport would require an enormous amount of research.

The alphabetical guide to every North Shields fishing vessel provides the following information.

(1) SN Number. It will be noted that the same registration number is often used two, three, or four times.

(2) Trawler Name. This is the name that the vessel held during its period of registration at North Shields.

(3) Time at North Shields. The dates shown are those during the period that the vessel was registered at North Shields up until 1967. If a single date is shown then the vessel was only there for that year. If a dash follows a single date the vessel was at North Shields after 1967.

(4) Type of Vessel. Refers to how the vessel was described in the Customs Records.

(5) When Built / Tonnage. The year when each trawler was built. Each trawler's gross tonnage is given to the nearest ton. Gross tonnage is

calculated from the cubic capacity of the vessel on the basis of one ton = 100 cubic feet. If either category of information is unknown this is shown as ****.

(6) History. This is the potted history of each individual vessel.

North Shields trawlers were lost all over the world but the most frequent area was in the bleak North Sea. The date when each trawler was lost is a key factor but it is likely that there will be slight variations in the date of the loss in official records and other reported dates in such documents as newspapers. The reason being that it was often the case that the loss of a trawler was not released for days and sometimes weeks after the actual event and even then it was surprisingly not always considered being newsworthy in the local press! On some occasions the date placed in the Customs registers against the word lost or missing is believed to be the date of the actual entry, the vessel having been missing for weeks or months.

In trying to provide specific locations many reference books have had to be researched. It is intended that the information given is factually correct but it is accepted that errors will occur. Obviously the author would be grateful to learn of any erroneous facts published.

Steam trawler in heavy seas.

North Shields Fishing Vessels

1352 *Achievement* (1884 Paddle Sloop) 1868 / 125t. Sank 9 miles East of Seaham on 23rd March 1884 after colliding with SS *Dunelm*.

98 *Admiral* (1891-1907 Dandy) 1890 / 103t. Recorded as foundered 1907.

1036 *Adonis* (1885-92 Paddle Sloop) 1873 / 78t. Ceased fishing.

84 *Advance* (1891 Ketch) 1890 / 60t. Wrecked on 14th November 1891 on the Black Midden Rocks at the mouth of the River Tyne.

1397 *Africa* (1883-91 Smack/Tug) 1883 / 122t. Reverted to tug duties.

224 *African Prince* (1898-1914 Trawler) 1896 / 125t. Transferred to Aberdeen as A114. Returned as SN 111.

111 *African Prince* (1928-31 Trawler) 1896 / 124t. On 19th June 1931 the vessel was lost in heavy seas. The location of the wreck (not positively identified) is 6 miles off Beadnell Point, Northumberland.

239 *Agnes* (1897-1917 Trawler) 1896 / 125t. In January 1917 lost in conflict. 9 crewmembers made prisoners of war.

187 *Agnes H Hastie* (1912-61 Trawler) 1912 / 209t. Ceased fishing – scrapped.

82 *Agnes S Walker* (1927-35 Trawler) 1917 / 227t. Transferred to Leith. Lost in 1942.

1092 *Alabama* (1881-83 Sail Lugger) 1839 / 29t. Transferred to Banff. Returned as SN 320.

320 *Alabama* (1904-11 Sail Lugger) 1839 / 29t. Ceased fishing.

375 *Albatross* (1918-20 Trawler) 1884 / 195t. On 19th June 1920 lost in unknown circumstances.

1438 *Albert Edward* (1887-90 Paddle Sloop) 1878 / 76t. Ceased fishing.

56 *Alex Hastie* (1914-41 Trawler) 1914 / 205t. Ceased fishing, scrapped.

81 *Alexandra* (1908-33 Ketch) 1904 / 181t. Scrapped.

136 *Alice Dodds* (1910-11 Ketch) 1910 / 196t. Wrecked on 27th February 1911 at North Ronaldsway.

24 *Alnwick Castle* (1899-1911 Drifter) 1895 / 96t. Transferred to Kirkcaldy as KY 120.

1456 *Alpha* (1885-89 Paddle Sloop) 1884 / 92t. Sank following a collision on 7th October 1889 with the *Lottie* in the North Sea.

11 *Ambassador* (1899-1910 Trawler) 1899 / 148t. Transferred to Dundee as DE 3.

92 *Amerique* (1960-67 Trawler) 1943 / 293t. Scrapped.

110 *Amy Gertrude* (1891-1906 Dandy) 1891 / 110t. Sold to the Netherlands.

1496 *Andrew Bain* (1887-1902 Paddle Sloop) 1885 / 129t. Sold to Gibraltar.

280 *Angelina* (1901 Trawler) 1901 / 186t. Transferred to Boston.

67 *Anglia* (1889-95 Dandy) 1885 / 58t. Sold to 'foreigners'.

251 *Anglia* (1900-15 Trawler) 1898 / 107t. Lost in conflict on 24th July 1915, 25 miles NWW of Sunlisker.

1183 *Annandale* (1888-90 Paddle Tug) 1869 / 66t. Reverted to tug duties.

172 *Annandale* (1894-1901 Paddle Sloop) 1893 / 129t. Sold to Russia.

SN 56 *Alex Hastie* at North Shields between 1914-41. Behind her lies SN 99 *Ben Torc*.

299 *Annie Anderson* (1916 Sail Lugger) **** / 77t. Vessel motorised. Lost in conflict on 5th July 1916, 16 miles ESE of Tynemouth.

149 *Annie Irvin* (1911-13 Trawler) 1911 / 186t. Sold to Capetown, South Africa.

1099 *Apollo* (1881-83 Paddle Sloop) 1856 / 16t. Customs register shows vessel lost at sea in 1883.

283 *Ariel Gazelle* (1901-08 Sail Lugger) **** / 20t. Scrapped.

86 *Arctic* (1900-07 Ketch) 1898 / 57t. Sold to Portugal.

169 *Arctic Prince* (1915-25 Trawler) 1915 / 194t. Transferred to Milford Haven.

5 *Athena* (1887-92 Drifter/Ketch) 1886 / 67t. Transferred to Rye.

260 *Atherine* (1898-1905 Trawler) 1898 / 145t. Recorded as lost in 1905, no other details available.

38 *Audrey* (1926-33 Ketch) 1906 / 186t. Lost on 6th September 1933, no other details known.

1500 *Australia* (1887-98 Paddle Tug) 1885 / 97t. Reverted to tug duties.

348 *Australian Prince* (1903-04 Trawler) 1903 / 157t. Sold to the Netherlands.

30 *Australian Prince* (1920-22 Trawler) 1919 / 202t. Strath class trawler 4423. Transferred to Grimsby as GY 239.

72 *Avacanora* (1908-17 Trawler) 1894 / 147t. Transferred to Aberdeen as A 838.

268 *Baden Powell* (1900-20 Trawler) 1900 / 93t. Lost in unknown circumstances on 11th February 1920.

233 *Bambro Castle* (1897-1907 Trawler) 1897 / 80t. Foundered after collision in 1907, no other details known.

152 *Bella* (1967- Motor Trawler) 1933 / 18t. Motor fishing vessel.

1152 *Belle* (1881-83 Sail Lugger) **** / 30t. Later registered as SN 1308.

1308 *Belle* (1884 Sail Lugger) **** / 30t. Later registered as SN 1425.

1425 *Belle* (1885-86 Sail Lugger) **** / 30t. Fate unknown.

136 *John Smart/Ben Aden* (1925-41 Trawler) 1918 / 203t. Strath class trawler 3635. Transferred to Milford Haven.

125 *Ben Arthur* (1914-60 Trawler) 1914 / 201t. Scrapped.

31 *Ben Bow* (1962- Motor Trawler) **** / ****. Motor fishing vessel.

20 *Ben Chourn* (1961- Motor Trawler) 1950 / 278t. Motor fishing vessel.

312 *Ben Earn* (1916-60 Trawler) 1916 / 235t. Scrapped.

110 *Ben Glamair* (1914-41 Trawler) 1914 / 197t. Lost in conflict on 17th July 1941 when the vessel went missing off Embleton Bay, Northumberland. 10 dead.

336 *Ben Glas* (1917-60 Trawler) 1917 / 234t. Scrapped.

SN 312 *Ben Earn* at North Shields for 44 years.

SN 137 *Ben Idris* – transferred to Granton.

SN 33 *Ben Vurie* in a heavy swell within the Tyne piers.

SN 269 *Ben Lora* – went to the scrapyard after 48 years service.

SN 68 *Cariama* and SN 310 *Shamrock*.

41 *Ben Glas* (1964- Motor Trawler) 1961 / 219t. Motor fishing vessel.

114 *Ben Hope* (1932-55 Trawler) 1917 / 202t. Strath class trawler 3631. Scrapped.

192 *Ben Idris* (1912-13 Trawler) 1897 / 124t. Sold to France.

137 *Ben Idris* (1932-45 Trawler) 1931 / 232t. Transferred to Granton as GN 7.

269 *Ben Lora* (1913-61 Trawler) 1913 / 197t. Scrapped.

43 *Ben Lora* (1964- Motor Trawler) 1961 / 219t. Motor fishing vessel.

340 *Ben Medie* (1917-58 Trawler) 1917 / 234t. On 8th October 1958 vessel totally lost, no other details known.

61 *Ben Roy* (1931-45 Trawler) 1929 / 259t. Transferred to Aberdeen.

78 *Ben Screel* (1936-42 Trawler) 1914 / 194t. Lost in conflict on 25th December 1942 off St Abbs Head, Scotland.

85 *Ben Strome* (1964- Motor Trawler) 1962 / ****. Motor fishing vessel.

99 *Ben Torc* (1936-48/1954-57 Trawler) 1915 / 199t. Scrapped.

100 *Ben Tore* (1960- Motor Trawler) **** / ****. Motor fishing vessel.

33 *Ben Vurie* (1967- Motor Trawler) **** / ****. Motor fishing vessel. Now scrapped.

113 *Ben Vurie* (1914-58 Trawler) 1914 / 200t. Scrapped.

199 *Bernicia* (1895-1900 Trawler) 1894 / 90t. Vessel went missing in the North Sea on 15th February 1900. 8 dead.

130 *Black Prince* (1892-1903 Schooner) 1892 / 125t. Stranded and lost on 16th November 1903 near Aberdeen.

1452 *Black Watch* (1884-1901 Paddle Sloop) 1884 / 84t. Reverted to tug duties.

36 *Blacktail* (1964-65 Motor Trawler) 1961 / 246t. Transferred to Lowestoft as LT 502 *Farnham Queen*.

221 *Blanche* (1887-97 Paddle Tug) 1873 / 78t. Foundered in 1897, no other details available.

1495 *Blucher* (1887-88 Paddle Smack) 1885 / 106t. Transferred to Grangemouth.

1405 *Blue Bonnet* (1885-90 Paddle Tug) 1847 / 63t. Ceased fishing.

1168 *Bonito* (1881-84 Trawler) 1878 / 98t. Transferred to Aberdeen.

34 *Boy Ernest* (1914-35 Ketch) 1902 / 55t. Scrapped.

288 *Boy Stanley* (1917 Sail Lugger) **** / 15t. Foundered and lost in 1917, no other details available.

1513 *British Prince* (1887-93 Trawler) 1885 / 46t. Sold to 'foreigners'.

288 *Britons Pride* (1917 Sail Lugger) **** / 15t. Ceased fishing.

90 *Britannia* (1890-94 Paddle Ketch) 1862 / 63t. Sold to Spain.

1406 *Brothers* (1888-91 Sail Lugger) 1873 / 35t. Ceased fishing.

222 *Caledonia* (1898-1903 Sail Keelboat) **** / 15t. Ceased fishing.

85 *Cambria* (1890-1911 Trawler) 1890 / 105t. Ceased fishing.

282 *Campania* (1901 Trawler) 1901 / 119t. Transferred to Aberdeen as A 486. Lost in 1904.

274 *Campville* (1900-05 Trawler) 1900 / 117t. Foundered in 1901. No other details available

349 *Canadian Prince* (1903-04 Trawler) 1903 / 158t. Sold to the Netherlands.

141 *Capella* (1892-97 Trawler) 1892 / 111t. Transferred to Dundee as DE 31.

68 *Cariama* (1902-13 Trawler) 1890 / 164t. Transferred to Liverpool as LL 166. Later sold to Greece.

335 *Celtic Prince* (1902-04 Trawler) 1902 / 155t. Sold to the Netherlands.

1398 *Challenge* (1885-1903 Paddle Sloop) 1861 / 76t. Foundered on 26th September 1903 off Blyth.

59 *Chancellor* (1889-1900 Trawler) 1889 / 78t. Transferred to Peterhead as PD 379.

279 *Chancellor* (1901-11 Trawler) 1901 / 168t. Transferred to Aberdeen as A 423

118 *Chris* (1910-31 Drifter) 1910 / 80t. Transferred to Banff as BF 263 *Rambler Rose*. Seen in 1997 at Hamburg. Believed to be still afloat.

29 *Christana T Purdy* (1921-62 Trawler) 1917 / 213t. Strath class trawler 3618. Scrapped.

294 *Cissy* (1901-19 Drifter) 1901 / 60t. Transferred to Buckie as BCK 331.

162 *COJ* (1911-12 Whaler) 1911 / 99t. Registration cancelled as vessel fishing abroad.

31 *Columbus* (1889-91 Paddle Trawler) 1865 / 73t. Ceased fishing.

1322 *Confidence* (1885-86 Paddle Sloop) 1857 / 69t. Transferred to Grimsby.

1089 *Conquest* (1885-1900 Paddle Sloop) 1866 / 72t. Sank on 39th May 1900, 10 miles ENE of Tynemouth.

1292 *Content* (1882-86 Sail Lugger) **** / 15t. Later registered as SN 1477.

SN 29 *Christania T Purdy* leaving the Tyne.

1477 *Content* (1887-1896 Sail Lugger) **** / 15t. Scrapped.

1408 *Contest* (1883-85 Paddle Tug) 1866 / 87t. Reverted to tug duties.

157 *Copieux* (1933-38 Trawler) 1918 / 202t. Strath class trawler 4415. Transferred to Aberdeen as A 465.

153 *Coquet* (1892-1912 Trawler) 1892 / 76t. Sold to France.

109 *Coral Isle* (1947-48 Trawler) 1917 / 323t. Mersey class trawler 3549. Transferred to Hull.

22 *Coral Isle* (1957- Drifter) **** / ****. Motor drifter.

376 *Cormorant IV* (1920-22 Trawler) 1897 / 161t. Transferred to Grimsby as GY 126.

337 *Coronatia* (1902-17 Trawler) 1902 / 184t. Transferred to Granton.

1173 *Courier* (1878-81 Paddle Tug) 1853 / 76t. Later registered as SN 1330.

1330 *Courier* (1883-86 Paddle Tug) 1853 / 76t. Later registered as SN 1438 and renamed *Albert Edward*.

8 *Cradock* (1934-41 Trawler) 1919 / 203t. Strath class trawler 4472. Lost in conflict on 8th November 1941, 14 miles NNE of St Abbs Head.

273 *Cragside* (1900-11 Trawler) 1900 / 114t. Foundered on 22nd July 1911 off Scotland.

266 *Craigelachie* (1899-1931 Trawler) 1896 / 111t. Scrapped.

135 *Crater* (1925-26 Trawler) 1896 / 153t. Foundered on 2nd June 1926, 6 miles East of Souter Lighthouse.

1155 *Croft* (1881 Sail Ketch) 1878 / 82t. Transferred to Hull.

92 *Crown Prince* (1890-1906 Trawler) 1890 / 109t. Transferred to Fraserburgh.

161 *Cruiser* (1893-98 Paddle Sloop) 1882 / 92t. Ceased fishing.

301 *Crystal* (1901-08 Drifter) 1901 / 73t. Wrecked on 5th December 1908 at Scorby Sands, Great Yarmouth.

46 *CSD* (1920-24 Drifter) 1919 / 96t. Transferred to Fraserburgh.

43 *Current* (1920-22 Ketch) 1919 / 96t. Transferred to Kirkcaldy.

330 *Cygnet* (1917-19 Trawler) 1893 / 138t. Transferred to Yarmouth as YH 127.

99 *Daisy* (1891-1912 Trawler) 1891 / 118t. Sold to Spain.

126 *Daisy* (1900-16 Drifter) 1900 / 54t. Transferred to Yarmouth.

11 *Danish Prince* (1888-89 Ketch) 1886 / ****. Lost off Souter Point on 26th March 1889 with all hands.

1381 *Dauntless* (1884-93 Paddle Tug) 1883 / 87t. Lost on 8th November 1893 off Thurso.

321 *Dependent* (1902 Sail Lugger) **** / 21t. Transferred to Wick.

1399 *Derwent* (1885-89 Paddle Sloop) 1860 / 67t. Scrapped.

315 *Dickson* (1904-14 Sail Lugger) **** / 26t. Customs records show vessel as wrecked. No other details.

81 *Digby Grand* (1890-97 Paddle Sloop) 1890 / 103t. Vessel lost, no known details.

SN 337 *Coronatia* – transferred to Granton in 1917.

48 *Dilston Castle* (1900-17 Trawler) 1900 / 129t. Lost in conflict on 17th May 1917, 16 miles ESE of Aberdeen.

49 *Dorade* (1964-65 Motor Trawler) 1961 / 246t. Transferred to Lowestoft as LT 503 *Oulton Queen*.

132 *Dorileen* (1947-57 Trawler) 1917 / 227t. Strath class trawler 3646. Scrapped.

61 *Doris* (1907-19 Trawler) 1907 / 82t. Transferred to Buckie as BCK 325.

302 *Dorothy* (1901-18 Drifter) 1901 / 60t. Transferred to Peterhead as PD 109.

1505 *Duchess* (1888-1904 Paddle Smack) 1886 / 104t. Scrapped.

34 *Earl of Windsor* (1889-92 Paddle Tug) 1873 / 85t. Wrecked on 20th October 1892 at Amble, Northumberland.

295 *Edith* (1901-11 Drifter) 1901 / 67t. Transferred to Peterhead as PD 99.

129 *Edith M Purdy* (1923-60 Trawler) 1918 / 205t. Strath class trawler 3748. Transferred to Aberdeen.

3 *Egyptian Prince* (1899-1916 Trawler) 1899 / 129t. Lost in conflict on 5th August 1916, 12 miles SSE of Longstone Light.

32 *Ekede* (1963- Motor Trawler) **** / ****. Motor fishing vessel.

1394 *Electric* (1883-93 Paddle Tug) 1883 / 94t. Ceased fishing.

61 *Emerald* (1889-95 Ketch) 1889 / 47t. Transferred to Kirkcaldy.

73 *Energy* (1889-99 Trawler) 1889 / 84t. Sold to Spain.

286 *English Prince* (1901-13 Trawler) 1903 /164t. Vessel sank following a collision on 24th August 1913, no other details known.

272 *Ethel* (1900-14 Trawler) 1900 / 58t. Transferred to Preston.

323 *Ethelbald* (1904-16 Trawler) 1902 / 94t. Sank following a collision on 4th August 1916. No other details available.

309 *Ethelbert* (1901-09 Trawler) 1901 / 92t. Transferred to Leith.

344 *Ethelwulf* (1903-18 Trawler) 1903 / 184t. Lost in conflict on 1st December 1918. 8 dead.

227 *Ethnee* (1913-18 Dandy) 1913 / 86t. Wrecked on 5th January 1918 on Goodwin Sands near the Fork Light.

62 *Evelina* (1930-39 Trawler) 1919 / 202t. Lost in conflict on 14th December 1939. 9 dead. Wreck believed to be off Souter Lighthouse, South Shields.

354 *Evelyn* (1903-08 Trawler) 1903 / 61t. Sold to Capetown, South Africa.

198 *Evelyn Joyce* (1915-24 Trawler) 1912 / 93t. Lost in the North Sea on 14th April 1924, no further details known.

328 *Excel* (1917 Ketch) 1895 / 156t. Lost in conflict on 12th February 1917, 53 miles NE of Tynemouth.

1467 *Expert* (1884-86 Paddle Sloop) 1856 / 52t. Recorded as lost in 1886, no other details known.

1410 *Fearless* (1884-90 Paddle Sloop) 1883 / 90t. Transferred to Scarborough as SH 186.

73 *Felicia* (1908-17 Trawler) 1908 / 74t. Transferred to Yarmouth as YH 633.

1468 *Fiery Dragon* (1887-90 Paddle Sloop) 1869 / 72t. Scrapped.

225 *Fisher Prince* (1897-1915 Trawler) 1896 / 125t. Transferred to Grimsby as GY 656. Lost in conflict 24th September 1916, 20 miles NE of Scarborough.

120 *Flixton* (1941-48 Trawler) 1919 / 201t. Strath class trawler 3816. Sold to Norway.

1 *Flying Arrow* (1887-1903 Paddle Tug) 1875 / 123t. Reverted to tug duties.

1181 *Flying Huntsman* (1880 Paddle Tug) 1863 / 128t. Lost on 28th October 1880 whilst entering the Tyne. 13 dead.

1218 *Flying Scotchman* (1887 Paddle Tug) 1876 / 50t. Reverted to tug use.

142 *Flying Spray* (1892-97 Paddle Sloop) 1876 / 87t. Transferred to Scarborough as SH 259.

244 *Foresters* (1899-1912 Sail Lugger) **** / 17t. Ceased fishing.

285 *Forth* (1916 Trawler) 1899 / 167t. Transferred to Grimsby as GY 1000. Lost in 1917.

1117 *Fury* (1881-1884 Paddle Sloop) 1857 / 69t. Re-registered and re-named SN 1322 *Confidence*.

95 *Gannet* (1890-1916 Trawler) 1890 / 63t. Transferred to Yarmouth as YH 450.

170 *GDI* (1911-12 Whaler) 1911 / 99t. Registration closed as permanently fishing abroad.

1180 *Gem* (1885-1897 Paddle Sloop) 1866 / 80t. Ceased fishing.

123 *General Joffre* (1914-51 Trawler) 1914 / 194t. Transferred to Milford Haven as M 158 *Southleigh*.

324 *George E Benson* (1904-17 Trawler) 1902 / 153t. Lost in conflict on 4th August 1916 in the North Sea. 9 men made prisoners of war.

44 *George Baird* (1888-97 Smack) 1888 / 66t. Sold to 'foreigners'.

274 *George H Hastie* (1916-57 Trawler) 1916 / 229t. Foundered on 9th December 1958 on the Island of Amrun en route to the breakers.

57 *George R Purdy* (1921-47 Trawler) 1917 / 212t. Strath class trawler 3617. Transferred to Plymouth as Bruce Sanger. Returned as SN 57 *Nigg Bay*.

270 *George Scott* (1916-54 Trawler) 1916 / 208t. Scrapped.

5 *Gillian* (1934-58 Trawler) 1919 / 205t. Strath class trawler 3853. Scrapped.

19 *Girl Irene* (1962- Motor Trawler) **** / ****. Motor fishing vessel.

1515 *Gleaner* (1887-91 Trawler) **** / 75t. Transferred to Swansea.

157 *Glenavon* (1893-95 Trawler) 1893 / 79t. Stranded and lost on 19th November 1895 off Boulmer, Northumberland.

196 *Glencona* (1894-1917 Trawler) 1894 / 78t. Transferred to Lowestoft as LT 179.

265 *Glendoon* (1898-1904 Trawler) 1898 / 117t. Transferred to Sunderland.

270 *Glenesk* (1900-04 Trawler) 1900 / 159t. Stranded and lost. No other details available.

51 *Graces* (1890-91 Sailing Lugger) **** / 20t. Fate unknown.

4 *Grecian Prince* (1899-1918 Trawler) 1899 / 126t. Lost in conflict on 17th December 1918 after hitting mine.

67 *Green Cormorant* (1962- Motor Trawler) 1956 / 21t. Motor fishing vessel.

21 *Guillemot* (1887-91 Ketch) 1887 / 53t. Lost in unknown circumstances on 22nd November 1891.

42 *Gulf Stream* (1920-24 Trawler) 1919 / 95t. Admiralty steel drifter 4167. Sold and re-registered SN 21 *Jenny Irvin*.

334 *Halcyon* (1917-19 Trawler) 1893 / 140t. Transferred to Yarmouth as YH 113.

SN 5 *Gillian* under her previous registration as LO 38 *Tom Jenkerson*. She was scrapped in 1958.

96 *Hamlet* (1923 Trawler) 1906 / 328t. Transferred to South Africa. Lost in 1927.

84 *Hans Tausen* (1964-65 Motor Trawler) **** / ****. Motor fishing vessel.

340 *Harfat Castle* (1902 Trawler) 1902 / 191t. Transferred to London.

34 *Harmony* (1902-07 Sail Lugger) **** / 20t. Ceased fishing.

1516 *Hartland* (1886-96 Paddle Sloop) 1870 / 87t. Transferred to Scarborough as SH 237.

1097 *Helen McGregor* (1881-83 Paddle Sloop) **** / 70t. Fate unknown.

370 *Hephzibah* (1918-20 Sail Lugger) 1891 / 42t. Ceased fishing.

1458 *Her Majesty* (1887 Paddle Sloop) 1865 / 94t. Foundered on 20th August 1887 at the mouth of the Tyne.

1144 *Heroine* (1881-82 Decked Boat) **** / 17t. Transferred to Anstruther.

150 *Hibernia* (1892-1915 Trawler) 1892 / 94t. Transferred to Lerwick as LK 257.

336 *Highland Prince* (1902-04 Trawler) 1902 / 158t. Sold to the Netherlands.

30 *Hindustan* (1899-1908 Trawler) 1895 / 150t. Foundered on 4th February 1908 in unknown circumstances.

222 *Honor* (1913-14 Trawler) 1913 / 71t. Transferred to Berwick as BK 22.

1393 *Hope* (1884-85 Sail Lugger) **** / 15t. Ceased fishing.

74 *Hopeful* (1954-55 Motor Trawler) **** / ****. Motor fishing vessel.

1098 *Hutchinson Hadaway* (1881-83 Sail Lugger) **** / 15t. Later registered as SN 1202.

1202 *Hutchinson Hadaway* (1883-85 Sail Lugger) **** / 15t. Ceased fishing.

312 *Ich Dien* (1901-05 Trawler) 1901 / 155t. Sold to the Netherlands.

1118 *Imperial Prince* (1881-83 Paddle Tug) 1858 / 63t. In 1883 the vessel was abandoned whilst fishing and sank.

26 *Imperial Prince* (1899-1914 Trawler) 1899 / 125t. Transferred to Aberdeen as A 145. Lost on 19th October 1923.

201 *Indian Prince* (1895-97 Trawler) 1895 / 129t. Wrecked on 29th March 1897 at the mouth of the River Tyne.

66 *Irene* (1907-14 Trawler) 1907 / 89t. Transferred to Berwick as BK 23, returned as SN 2.

2 *Irene* (1919-20 Trawler) 1907 / 89t. Transferred to Buckie as BCK 341.

285 *Irish Prince* (1901-07 Trawler) 1901 / 163t. Custom records show vessel as stranded and lost, no other details.

16 *Iron King* (1888-89 Paddle Trawler) 1880 / 112t. Wrecked on 3rd January 1889, 5 miles South of Scarborough.

105 *Isa* (1914-31 Ketch) 1914 / 86t. Transferred to Fraserburgh.

148 *Island Prince* (1912-22 Trawler) 1911 / 200t. Transferred to Aberdeen. Returned as SN 53.

53 *Island Prince* (1927 Trawler) 1911 / 200t. Lost on 6th September 1927 in unknown circumstances.

1160 *Isle of Cyprus* (1881 Sail Lugger) **** / 20t. Later registered as SN 1286.

1286 *Isle of Cyprus* (1882-96 Sail Lugger) **** / 20t. Scrapped.

53 *Ivernia* (1900-14 Trawler) 1900 / 155t. Sold to Turkey.

40 *J G Allison* (1934-58 Liddock Trawler) 1919 / 202t. Scrapped.

193 *J H Mould* (1894-1907 Paddle Sloop) 1894 / 126t. Transferred to South Shields.

1383 *James* (1884-96 Sail Lugger) **** / 15t. Transferred to Kirkcaldy.

172 *James Pitcher* (1911-22 Trawler) 1911 / 197t. Ceased fishing.

76 *Jason* (1909-15 Trawler) 1898 / 175t. Lost in conflict on 1st April 1915, 40 miles NNE of Tynemouth.

1277 *Jasper* (1885-97 Paddle Sloop) 1870 / 85t. Scrapped.

21 *Jeanie Irvin* (1926-47 Trawler) 1919 / 95t. Admiralty drifter 4167. Sold to Poland. Later registered at Lowestoft LT 57.

18 *Jennie Stewart* (1920-38 Trawler) 1916 / 211t. Lost in the North Sea 25th December 1938. 11 dead.

180 *Jocelyn* (1915-27 Dandy) 1915 / 93t. Transferred to Peterhead as PD 154.

133 *John Bennett* (1928-29 Trawler) 1915 / 228t. Sold to the Netherlands.

70 *John C Meikle* (1914-19 Trawler) 1914 / 193t. Sold to Capetown.

142 *John C Meikle* (1910-14 / 1920-24 Trawler) 1910 / 198t. Transferred to Aberdeen as A 51 Craigendarroch. Returned in 1920. Lost on 31st July 1924, 6 miles South of Aberdeen. No fatalities.

52 *John Donovan* (1914-58 Trawler) 1914 / 205t. Scrapped.

69 *John Fitzgerald* (1921-41 Trawler) 1918 / 234t. Transferred to Aberdeen.

305 *John G Watson* (1904-24 Trawler) 1916 / 234t. Sank on 20th May 1930, 9 miles North of the Farne Islands.

35 *John Hedley* (1920-25 Trawler) 1918 / 95t. Admiralty steam drifter 3877. Transferred to Inverness as INS 55 *Preeminent*.

233 *John High* (1916 Trawler) 1916 / 228t. Lost in conflict on 7th August 1916 off Mount Sozonova in the White Sea. 2 dead.

138 *John Jackson* (1928-33 Trawler) 1919 / 202t. Strath class trawler 3847. Transferred to Aberdeen as A 265 *Inchgower*. Returned to North Shields in 1950 retaining Aberdeen number. Lost in 1953.

111 *John M Smart* (1891-1917 Trawler) 1891 / 113t. Lost in conflict on 12th December 1917, 10 miles East of the River Tyne. 2 dead.

263 *Kate* (1901-11 Sail Lugger) **** / 20t. Scrapped.

63 *Keilder Castle* (1900-17 Trawler) 1900 / 129t. Transferred to Fleetwood as FD 40.

42 *Kendale* (1958-62 Trawler) 1930 / 243t. Previously SN 107. Scrapped.

332 *King Edward* (1902-10 Trawler) 1902 / 208t. Transferred to Cardiff.

236 *Kirklinton* (1916 Trawler) 1916 / 226t. Transferred to Fleetwood as FD 293.

25 *Kittiwake* (1887-99 Dandy) 1887 / 53t. Transferred to Aberdeen.

308 *Kitty* (1901-13 Drifter) 1901 / 56t. Transferred to Peterhead as PD 103.

154 *L H Rutherford* (1934-37 Trawler) 1917 / 247t. Sold to Norway.

98 *Lady Edith* (1964- Motor Trawler) **** / ****. Motor fishing vessel.

248 *Lanercost* (1916 Trawler) 1916 / 226t. Transferred to Fleetwood as FD 292.

89 *Langley Castle* (1900-16 Trawler) **** / 93t. Lost in conflict on 14th July 1916, 18 miles NEE of Tynemouth.

257 *Laureate* (1898-1911 Trawler) 1898 / 190t. Sold to Portugal. Returned as SN 237.

237 *Laureate* (1913-19 Trawler) 1898 / 193t. Transferred to Fleetwood as FD 35.

1272 *Leading Star* (1885-89 Paddle Tug) 1872 / 76t. Wrecked on 19th August 1889, 4 miles North of Scarborough.

11 *Leam / Belldock* (1934-41 Trawler) 1917 / 235t. Transferred to Grimsby as GY 367. Lost in 1953.

45 *Leonard Boyle* (1920-26 Drifter) 1919 / 96t. Admiralty steel drifter 4149. Transferred to Fraserburgh.

37 *Lerita* (1914-31 Dandy) 1914 / 79t. Transferred to Fraserburgh as FR 197.

88 *Lillian Maud* (1890-1900 Dandy) 1890 / 57t. Transferred to Peterhead.

79 *Lillie* (1890-1912 Trawler) 1890 / 81t. Scrapped.

348 *Lilly* (1917-19 / 1923-31 Sail Lugger) **** / 19t. Transferred to Dundee and then returned. Scrapped.

50 *Lily* (1888-1913 Paddle Sloop) 1888 / 127t. Wrecked on 15th April 1911 at Seaton Sluice, Northumberland.

275 *Lily* (1900-14 Trawler) 1900 / 71t. Lost in conflict on 8th October 1914, 28 miles ENE of Tynemouth.

38 *Lilydale* (1899-1915 Trawler) 1899 / 128t. Lost in conflict on 28th April 1915, 37 miles East of St Abbs Head, Scotland.

1120 *Lion* (1881-82 Paddle Sloop) 1858 / 74t. Later registered as SN 1291.

SN 14 *Lowdock* originally named *Peter Lovett*.

1291 *Lion* (1882-84 Paddle Sloop) 1858 / 74t. Later registered as SN 1328.

1328 *Lion* (1885 Paddle Sloop) 1858 / 74t. Later registered as SN 1364.

1364 *Lion* (1886 Paddle Sloop) 1858 / 74t. Ceased fishing.

109 *Lionel* (1891-1915 Paddle Tug) 1891 / 122t. Reverted to tug use.

1428 *Little John* (1884-86 Paddle Sloop) **** / ****. Foundered on 13th January 1886 in the River Tyne.

1463 *Lizard* (1881-91 Paddle Sloop) 1869 / 82t. Transferred to Middlesbrough.

84 *Lizzie* (1966- Motor Trawler) **** / ****. Motor fishing vessel.

296 *Lizzie* (1917-18 Sail Lugger) **** / 17t. Fitted with auxiliary motor. Transferred to Bridlington.

104 *Londonderry* (1891-93 Schooner) 1891 / 439t. Sold to France.

287 *Loraine* (1916-19 Trawler) 1916 / 95t. Sold to the Admiralty.

159 *Lord Stanley* (1893 / 1895-1900 Paddle Sloop) 1873 / 92t. Initially named *Glenbervie*. Scrapped.

267 *Lottie* (1900-16 Drifter) 1900 / 59t. Transferred to Yarmouth as YH 430.

184 *Lottie Leash* (1912-15 Trawler) 1907 / 93t. Lost in conflict on 18th January 1915 off Saseno Island.

14 *Lowdock* (1934-40 Trawler) 1917 / 175t. Castle class trawler 3509. Initially named *Peter Lovett*. Sank following a collision on 19th March 1940.

244 *Loyal Prince* (1913-29 Trawler) 1913 / 208t. Transferred to Aberdeen as A 376.

108 *Lucania* (1901-16 Trawler) 1900 / 92t. Lost in conflict on 3rd August 1916, 7 miles ENE of Coquet Island.

SN 244 *Loyal Prince*.

152 *M A Dodds* (1892-1918 Trawler) 1892 / 150t. Transferred to Lowestoft as LT 645.

26 *M A Southern* (1962- Motor Trawler) 1958 / 24t. Motor fishing vessel.

160 *Margaret Clark* (1967- Motor Trawler) **** / ****. Motor fishing vessel.

72 *Marie Roze* (1889-1900 Dandy) 1889 / 56t. Foundered according to Custom records, no further details available.

107 *Marjory M Hastie* (1930-42 Trawler) 1930 / 1942. Transferred to Glasgow. Returned as SN 42 *Kendale*.

327 *Mary* (1901-14 Drifter) 1902 / 65t. Transferred to Peterhead as PD 161.

36 *Mary A Hastie* (1926-30 Trawler) 1913 / 248t. Initially called *Onyx* 11. Sold abroad. Returned as SN 96.

96 *Mary A Hastie* (1932-46 Trawler) 1930 / 243t. Transferred to Glasgow.

1440 *Mary Usher* (1885-86 Paddle Tug) 1866 / 87t. Later registered as SN 3.

3 *Mary Usher* (1887-88 Paddle Tug) 1866 / 87t. Ceased fishing.

23 *Mauveen* (1920-31 Trawler) 1918 / 95t. Transferred to Banff.

1444 *May* (1888-99 Paddle Tug) 1870 / 67t. Foundered on 10th May 1899.

175 *Mayflower* (1893-1917 Trawler) 1893 / 85t. Transferred to Peterhead as PD 298.

253 *Merchant Prince* (1900-16 Trawler) 1898 / 130t. Lost in conflict on 3rd August 1916, 14 miles SE of the Farne Islands.

250 *Mercia* (1900-12 Trawler) 1898 / 93t. Sold to France.

1347 *Minnie* (1883-92 Sail Lugger) **** / 15t. Scrapped.

303 *Minnie* (1901-07 Drifter) 1901 / 62t. Transferred to Fraserburgh as FR 210.

192 *Mizpah* (1894-1900 Trawler) 1894 / 165t. Recorded as missing in 1900, register closed on 28th March 1900.

64 *Morning Star* (1889-96 Ketch) 1889 / 63t. Sold to Spain.

25 *Morning Star* (1925-37 Trawler) 1900 / 145t. Scrapped.

163 *Nancy* (1901-19 Trawler) 1900 / 59t. Lost on 17th November 1919, no other details known.

154 *Nancy Hunnam* (1892-1916 Ketch) 1892 / 57t. Lost in conflict on 6th July 1916, 24 miles ESE of the River Tyne.

252 *Naval Prince* (1900-18 Trawler) 1898 / 130t. Lost on 10th December 1915, no other details known.

103 *Nellie* (1891-98 Trawler) 1891 / 112t. Wrecked on 24th March 1898 at Peterhead. 8 dead.

254 *Nellie* (1898-1915 Trawler) 1898 / 109t. Lost in conflict on 1st April 1915, 35 miles NE of Tynemouth.

159 *Nellie Dodds* (1911-19 Trawler) 1911 / 220t. Fate unknown.

108 *Nellie Wilson* (1927-37 Trawler) 1910 / 198t. Scrapped.

350 *Nelly* (1903-19 Drifter) 1903 / 75t. Sold to Admiralty.

1000 *Nelson* (1881-83 Keelboat) **** / 25t. Later registered as SN 1255.

1255 *Nelson* (1883-85 Keelboat) **** / 25t. Later registered as SN 1275.

1275 *Nelson* (1886 Keelboat) **** / 25t. Fate unknown.

36 *New Century* (1907-14 Ketch) 1906 / 143t. Sold to Turkey.

32 *New Enterprise* (1906-14 Trawler) 1901 / 145t. Sold to Turkey.

229 *Newark Castle* (1913-16 Trawler) 1897 / 85t. Lost in conflict on 6th July 1916, 23 miles SE of Tynemouth.

57 *Nigg Bay* (1954-62 Trawler) 1906 / 237t. Previously SN 57 *George R Purdy*. Scrapped.

130 *Noblese* (1965-66 Motor trawler) **** / ****. Motor fishing vessel.

90 *Norbreck* (1922-26 Trawler) 1905 / 200t. Transferred to Aberdeen as A 164 *Glenstar*.

44 *Noreen* (1914-25 Dandy) 1914 / 79t. Lost on 2nd November 1925 in unknown circumstances.

3 *Norham Castle* (1899-1913 Trawler) 1899 / 93t. Transferred to Peterhead. Returned as SN 35.

35 *Norham Castle* (1919-20 Trawler) 1899 / 93t. Vessel lost on 20th October 1920 in unknown circumstances.

20 *Norman* (1924 Sailing Trawler) 1912 / 20t. Transferred to Campbletown.

1485 *Norman Prince* (1885-99 Paddle Sloop) 1885 / 87t. Ceased fishing.

48 *Norstaw* (1958- Trawler) 1957 / 38t. Motor fishing vessel.

282 *Northern Prince* (1914-19 Trawler) 1913 / 207t. Transferred to Whitby as WY 40.

168 *Northumbria* (1893-1916 Trawler) 1893 / 81t. Transferred to London.

90 *Nunthorpe Hall* (1909 Trawler) 1909 / 248t. Purchased by the Admiralty, never used for fishing.

112 *Ocean Prince* (1891-96 Trawler) 1891 / 127t. Wrecked at Collieston, Scotland, on 11th December 1896.

42 *Olden Times* (1934-50 Trawler) 1919 / 202t. Strath class trawler 425. Scrapped.

174 *Orcadia* (1893-1906 Trawler) 1893 / 82t. Transferred to Aberdeen.

102 *Pansy* (1891-97 Trawler) 1891 / 112t. Stranded and lost near Montrose on 27th July 1897.

1112 *Patriot* (1881 Paddle Tug) 1867 / 91t. Later registered as SN 1412.

1412 *Patriot* (1883-1901 Paddle Tug) 1867 / 91t. Scrapped.

71 *Pelamid* (1965-66 Motor Trawler) **** / ****. Motor fishing vessel.

1497 *Pera* (1887-89 Paddle Sloop) 1885 / 107t. Sold to 'foreigners'.

80 *Pero Gomez* (1890-1900 Paddle Tug) 1869 / 96t. Transferred to Bowness.

1083 *Pilot* (1881-85 Paddle Sloop) 1856 / 83t. Scrapped.

1492 *Pioneer* (1885-96 Dandy) 1885 / 47t. Sold to Spain.

171 *Polar Prince* (1915-58 Trawler) 1915 / 194t. Scrapped.

1402 *Powerful* (1884-93 Paddle Sloop) 1865 / 89t. Transferred to Alloa.

56 *Premier* (1890-1907 Trawler) 1889 / 88t. Transferred to Banff. Lost in January 1918 off Skye.

278 *Premier* (1901-13 Trawler) 1901 / 109t. Transferred to Aberdeen as A 471. Lost in 1915.

245 *Pretoria* (1900-19 Trawler) 1900 / 155t. Transferred to Fleetwood as FD 212.

1077 *Pride of the Ocean* (1881-83 Ketch) 1881 / 91t. Later registered as SN 1370.

1370 *Pride of the Ocean* (1884 Ketch) 1881 / 91t. Later registered as SN 1427.

1427 *Pride of the Ocean* (1885-97 Ketch) 1881 / 91t. Scrapped.

94 *Prima* (1891 Trawler) 1884 / 105t. Wrecked on 21st December 1891 at the mouth of the River Tyne.

115 *Primrose* (1893-99 Trawler) 1891 / 136t. Transferred to Dundee as DE 114.

27 *Prince Consort* (1897-1900 Paddle Sloop) 1874 / 125t. Sank following a collision on 16th August 1900 at the mouth of the Tyne.

15 *Princess Alice* (1914-18 Trawler) 1914 / 224t. Lost on 6th March 1918 following a collision off Alexandria, Egypt.

352 *Princess Beatrice* (1903-08 Trawler) 1903 / 203t. Sold to Spain.

202 *Princess Beatrice* (1913-14 Trawler) 1913 / 213t. Lost in conflict on 5th October 1914 off the coast of Belgium.

18 *Princess Louise* (1905-09 Trawler) 1905 / 250t. Sold to Spain.

27 *Princess Mary* (1914-29 Trawler) 1914 / 124t. Transferred to Granton as GN 11.

54 *Princess Maud* (1907-10 Trawler) 1906 / 269t. Sold to 'foreigners'.

334 *Princess May* (1902-08 Trawler) 1902 / 208t. Sold to Russia.

326 *Princess Olga* (1917-18 Trawler) 1916 / 244t. Lost in conflict on 14th June 1918 off Le Havre, France.

SN 351 *Princess Victoria* – sold to Portugal.

SN 246 *R Irvin* on sea trials.

45 *Princess Royal* (1906-09 Trawler) 1906 / 283t. Sold to 'foreigners'.

209 *Princess Royal* (1914-42 Trawler) 1913 / 213t. Transferred to Grimsby.

351 *Princess Victoria* (1903-13 Trawler) 1903 / 203t. Sold to Portugal.

321 *Princess Victoria* (1916-29 Trawler) 1916 / 244t. Transferred to Fleetwood as FD 50.

143 *Progress* (1892-95 Sailing Ketch) **** / 18t. Transferred to West Hartlepool.

158 *Progress* (1967- Motor Trawler) 1931 / 22t. Motor fishing vessel.

261 *Prudhoe Castle* (1898-1909 Trawler) 1898 / 84t. Transferred to Aberdeen.

333 *Queen Alexandra* (1902-12 Trawler) 1902 / 308t. Transferred to Dundee. Lost in conflict in 1915.

1299 *Quickstep* (1888-99 Paddle Sloop) 1877 / 91t. Lost in June 1889 off Souter Point.

83 *Quintia* (1914-31 Ketch) 1914 / 89t. Transferred to Fraserburgh as FR 205.

246 *R Irvin* (1913-19 Trawler) 1913 / 208t. Transferred to Whitby.

292 *Raider* (1913-14 Trawler) 1901 / 93t. Sold to Greece.

1045 *Rambler* (1884-86 Paddle Sloop) 1865 / 63t. Later registered as SN 1491.

1491 *Rambler* (1887-88 Paddle Sloop) 1865 / 63t. Ceased fishing.

247 *Rambler* (1898-1918 Trawler) 1898 / 92t. Lost in conflict on 26th February 1918, 4 miles East of Blyth. 9 dead.

256 *Ranger* (1898-1904 Trawler) 1898 / 93t. Sank on 26th January 1904 after a collision in the River Tyne.

1432 *Ranger* (1885-86 Paddle Sloop) 1866 / 64t. Later registered as SN 1508.

Two of the new breed of trawlers which only stayed a short time at North Shields before transferring to Hull.

SN 147 *Ranger Ajax*.

SN 149 *Ranger Aurora*.

1508 *Ranger* (1887-88 Paddle Sloop) 1866 / 64t. Ceased fishing.

147 *Ranger Ajax* (1967- Motor Trawler) 1965 / 776t. Motor fishing vessel.

148 *Ranger Apollo* (1967- Motor Trawler) 1965 / 778t. Motor fishing vessel. Transferred to Hull in 1973 as H 233 *Turcoman*.

149 *Ranger Aurora* (1967- Motor Trawler) 1966 / 779t. Motor fishing vessel. Transferred to Hull in 1973 as H 236 *Esquimaux*.

300 *Ranter* (1904-24 Trawler) 1901 / 99t. Lost on 27th August 1924, no other details known.

32 *Rapid* (1877-96 Paddle Tug) 1864 / 74t. Reverted to tug use.

1056 *Rapid* (1877-97 Paddle Sloop) 1868 / 90t. Transferred to Montrose.

104 *Rattray* (1909-20 Ketch) 1900 / 181t. Transferred to Grimsby as GY 720.

2 *Reaper* (1899-18 Trawler) 1889 / 91t. Lost during conflict on 21st February 1918. 8 dead.

94 *Reaver* (1900-01 Trawler) 1900 / 95t. Foundered on 25th January 1901 in the North Sea.

293 *Recorder* (1902-16 Trawler) 1901 / 149t. Lost in conflict on 14th July 1916, 18 miles NE of Tynemouth.

297 *Redvers Bullet* (1901-28 Trawler) 1901 / 99t. Scrapped.

8 *Rejoice* (1919-28 Trawler) 1915 / 82t. Foundered on 9th June 1928, 14 miles South East of River Tyne.

128 *Relko* (1964- Motor Trawler) **** / ****. Motor fishing vessel.

51 *Rene* (1915-31 Dandy) 1914 / 89t. Transferred to Fraserburgh as FR 220.

215 *Research* (1912-16 Ketch) 1902 / 57t. Transferred to Yarmouth as YH 421.

1174 *Restless* (1881-88 Paddle Sloop) 1857 / 68t. Ceased fishing.

18 *Retriever* (1889-1901 Trawler) 1899 / 92t. Lost off Grimsby between 12th-14th November 1901.

258 *Rhodesia* (1898-1916 Trawler) 1898 / 110t. Lost in conflict on 1st August 1916, 14 miles ESE of Tynemouth.

60 *Richmond Castle* (1907-20 Trawler) 1901 / 178t. Transferred to Dundee as DE 29.

121 *Right Way* (1932 Trawler) 1931 / 263t. Stranded and lost at Collieston, Scotland.

47 *Roamer* (1900-12 Trawler) 1900 / 93t. Lost on 11th July 1912 off Wick.

42 *Robert & Francis* (1889-1910 Sail Lugger) **** / 15t. Scrapped.

30 *Robert Gibson* (1929-33 Trawler) 1918 / 202t. Transferred to Aberdeen as A 228 *Corennie*. Went missing in May 1940.

189 *Robert Hastie* (1912-60 Trawler) 1912 / 209t. Scrapped.

45 *Rose* (1889-90 Trawler) 1888 / 79t. Sold to Portugal.

210 *Rose* (1895-1916 Trawler) 1895 / 96t. Transferred to Lowestoft as LT 1754.

211 *Rosslyn* (1915-16 Trawler) 1895 / 113t. Transferred to Scarborough.

240 *Rover* (1897-1901 Trawler) 1897 / 90t. Wrecked on 28th June 1901 off Souter Point.

SN 189 *Robert Hastie* – one of the longest serving SN trawlers.

1401 *Royal Dane* (1885-91 Paddle Sloop) 1864 / 72t. Ceased fishing.

287 *Royal Diadem* (1901-03 Sail Lugger) **** / 20t. Ceased fishing.

1290 *Royal Duke* (1887-1904 Paddle Sloop) 1873 / 107t. Scrapped.

70 *Royal Prince* (1889-1907 Smack) 1889 / 103t. Transferred to Leith.

74 *Ruby* (1890-1900 Dandy) 1889 / 58t. Transferred to Banff and renamed *Seagull*.

71 *Ruth Bolton* (1889-95 Dandy) 1889 / 72t. Sold to Spain.

58 *Sailfin* (1964-65 Motor Trawler) 1962 / 390t. Transferred to Lowestoft as LT 501 *Yoxford Queen*.

276 *Sailor Prince* (1901-14 Trawler) 1900 / 155t. Foundered in 1914. No other details available.

212 *Sapphire* (1895-1910 Trawler) 1895 / 77t. Foundered off Whitburn in 1910.

342 *Sara* (1902-13 Drifter) 1902 / 62t. Transferred to Peterhead as PD 100.

91 *Sarah* (1890-1901 Ketch) 1890 / 123t. Sold to Spain.

40 *Sarah* (1906-28 Trawler) 1899 / 135t. Wrecked on 30th April 1928 at Newbiggin.

4 *Sarah A Purdy* (1926-62 Trawler) 1919 / 202t. Strath class trawler 3774. Scrapped.

1327 *Sarah Ann* (1883-86 Keelboat) **** / 16t. Transferred to Kirkcaldy.

22 *Saxon* (1920-31 Trawler) 1894 / 118t. Foundered in the North Sea on 22nd April 1931.

1460 *Saxon Prince* (1884-1903 Paddle Smack) 1884 / 86t. Reverted to tug duties. Lost in 1907

58 *Saxon Prince* (1907-16 Trawler) 1906 / 237t. Lost on 28th March 1916 in a storm off Dover. 9 dead.

1518 *Scotia* (1886-1900 Trawler) 1886 / 55t. Transferred to Southampton as SU 11.

198 *Scotia* (1894-1907 Trawler) 1894 / 92t. Customs records show that vessel foundered after a collision in 1907.

1282 *Scotland* (1885-86 Paddle Sloop) 1878 / 77t. Later registered as SN 1418.

1418 *Scotland* (1886-89 Paddle Sloop) 1878 / 77t. Foundered March 1889, 20 miles East of Blyth. Crew rescued by SS *Libra*.

10 *Scotland* (1888-90 Paddle Tug) 1878 / 76t. Ceased fishing, scrapped in 1908.

190 *Scots Grey* (1894-1904 Trawler) 1894 / 76t. Transferred to Kirkcaldy.

28 *Scottish Prince* (1899-1913 Trawler) 1899 / 131t. Lost in conflict on 30th May 1913 off Holy Island.

54 *Scour* (1920-22 Drifter) 1919 / 98t. Transferred to Berwick.

12 *Yolanda* / *Sedock* (1934-42 Trawler) 1920 / 207t. Strath class trawler 4496. Transferred to Grimsby GY 123.

1113 *Selina* (1877-86 Paddle Tug) 1877 / 78t. Ceased fishing.

1476 *Selina* (1885-96 Paddle Sloop) 1870 / 66t. Ceased fishing.

1433 *Shamrock* (1884-1903 Paddle Sloop) 1870 / 108t. Ceased fishing.

310 *Shamrock* (1901-15 Trawler) 1901 / 157t. Transferred to Grimsby as GY 746.

171 *Sheldrake* (1893-1904 Trawler) 1893 / 95t. Vessel lost in unknown circumstances in 1904.

1239 *Silver Herring* (1887 Sail Ketch) 1868 / 21t. Customs register shows vessel as run down and wrecked, no other details.

1510 *Skylark* (1888-1905 Paddle Sloop) 1876 / 88t. Scrapped.

47 *Sleet* (1920-24 Drifter) 1918 / 97t. Admiralty steel drifter 3999. Transferred to Berwick as BK 5 *Eyedale*.

SN 4 *Sarah A Purdy* – scrapped in 1962.

SN 12 *Seddock* whilst under an Aberdeen registration.

277 *Soldier Prince* (1901-20 Trawler) 1900 / 155t. Sold to the Admiralty.

97 *Solveig* (1964-65 Motor Trawler) **** / ****. Motor fishing vessel.

121 *Southern Prince* (1915-21 Trawler) 1914 / 194t. Transferred to Sunderland.

185 *Southern Sea* (1912 Whaler) 1912 / 203t. Registration cancelled as vessel permanently fishing abroad.

186 *Southern Sky* (1912 Whaler) 1912 / 203t. Registration cancelled as vessel permanently fishing abroad.

208 *St Abbs* (1895-1912 Dandy) 1895 / 91t. Transferred to Lowestoft as LT 738.

88 *St Agnes No 1* (1908-48 Trawler) 1908 / 205t. Lost on 8th July 1948, no further details known.

49 *St George* (1906-15 Trawler) 1906 / 214t. Lost in conflict on 2nd May 1915, 65 miles ENE of Aberdeen.

1499 *St Giles* (1885-1904 Paddle Sloop) 1885 / 90t. Ceased fishing.

43 *St Gothard* (1900-13 Trawler) 1900 / 138t. Sold to the Netherlands.

102 *St Lawrence No 1* (1909-52 Trawler) 1909 / 211t. Scrapped.

217 *St Leonard No 1* (1913-41 Trawler) 1913 / 210t. Lost in conflict on 1st December 1941 after attack by enemy aircraft.

271 *St Louis* (1900-09 Trawler) 1900 / 135t. Recorded as foundered, register closed in 1909.

101 *St Louis No 1* (1909-15 Trawler) 1909 / 211t. Lost in conflict on 2nd May 1915, 50 miles ENE of May Island.

21 *St Olive* (1906-16 Trawler) 1906 / 201t. Lost in conflict on 5th August 1916, 11 miles East of Coquet Island.

47 *St Olive* (1935-55 Trawler) 1914 / 236t. Originally called *Noogana*. Scrapped.

1458 *St Oswin* (1885-1902 Paddle Sloop) 1884 / 90t. Ceased fishing.

45 *St Vincent* (1900-12 Trawler) 1900 / 137t. Sold to Portugal.

12 *Stag* (1885-1900 Paddle Tug) 1885 / 123t. Transferred to Sunderland.

1050 *Stanley* (1882-88 Paddle Sloop) 1868 / 91t. Later registered as SN 1053.

1053 *Stanley* (1882-88 Paddle Sloop) 1868 / 91t. Ceased fishing.

1280 *Star of Hope* (1885-91 Paddle Sloop) 1877 / 79t. Later registered as SN 149.

149 *Star of Hope* (1892-95 Paddle Sloop) 1877 / 79t. Ceased fishing.

1376 *Start* (1889 Paddle Tug) 1868 / 87t. Wrecked on 18th December 1893 near Leith.

8 *Stephenson* (1886-1913 Paddle Trawler) 1886 / 123t. Ceased fishing.

284 *Stirling Castle* (1901-12 Trawler) 1901 / 150t. Sold to the Netherlands.

36 *Storm King* (1888-1900 Paddle Sloop) 1864 / 136t. Ceased fishing.

71 *Success* (1908-10 Ketch) 1900 / 55t. Transferred to Lowestoft as LT 132.

1115 *Sunbeam* (1881-86 Paddle Tug) 1862 / 57t. Later registered as SN 1472.

1472 *Sunbeam* (1887-88 Paddle Tug) 1862 / 57t. Ceased fishing.

289 *Sunshine* (1901-21 Sail Lugger) **** / 15t. Ceased fishing.

255 *T W Mould* (1898-1910 Trawler) 1898 / 109t. Lost in conflict on 1st December 1918, 30 NE of Tynemouth. 10 dead.

148 *Teal Duck* (1892-99 Drifter) 1892 / 64t. Customs records show vessel as lost, no other details.

1037 *Teazer* (1885-86 Paddle Sloop) 1866 / 71t. Later registered as SN 1093.

1093 *Teazer* (1886-1900 Paddle Sloop) 1866 / 71t. Ceased fishing.

1038 *Terrible* (1877-88 Paddle Tug) 1866 / 85t. Foundered on 23rd August 1888 off Newbiggin by the Sea.

134 *The Way* (1931-35 Trawler) 1931 / 263t. Transferred to Aberdeen as A 336.

311 *Thistle* (1901-20 Trawler) 1901 / 158t. Transferred to Aberdeen.

265 *Thomas W Irwin* (1917-61 Trawler) 1916 / 209t. Scrapped.

143 *Thomas Young* (1910-14 Trawler) 1910 / 198t. Sold to Belgium.

67 *Thomas Young* (1914-19 Trawler) 1914 / 193t. Transferred to Hartlepool.

127 *Three Bells* (1957- Motor Trawler) **** / ****. Motor fishing vessel.

91 *Titania* (1909-12 Trawler) 1900 / 204t. Sold to 'foreigners'.

241 *Trawler Prince* (1897-1916 Trawler) 1897 / 126t. Lost in conflict on 3rd August 1916, 12 miles SSE of Longstone Light.

118 *Triumph* (1880 Paddle Tug) **** / ****. Ceased fishing.

41 *Tudor Prince* (1889-96 Smack) 1888 / 77t. Sold to the Isle of Man.

21 *Tudor Time* (1962- Trawler) 1957 / 19t. Motor vessel.

167 *TW1* (1911-12 Whaler) 1911 / 136t. Registration cancelled as permanently fishing abroad.

178 *Tweedside* (1893-1912 Trawler) 1893 / 79t. Sold to France.

180 *Tyne Belle* (1893-1905 Trawler) 1893 / 140t. Sold to Holland.

179 *Tyne Castle* (1893-1904 Trawler) 1893 / 140t. Sold to Holland.

1502 *Tyne Dale* (1885-1902 Paddle Smack) 1885 / 99t. Ceased fishing.

113 *Tyne Fisher* (1891-1907 Trawler) 1891 / 110t. Sold to Norway.

SN 265 *T W Irvin* being towed back to port after fouling her propeller.

145 *Tyne Meadows* (1893-1905 Trawler) 1892 / 139t. Sold to the Netherlands.

144 *Tyne Monarch* (1893-1905 Trawler) 1892 / 139t. Sold to the Netherlands.

97 *Tyne Prince* (1909-37 Trawler) 1909 / 205t. Scrapped.

125 *Tyne Stream* (1891-1906 Ketch) 1891 / 133t. Sold to Norway.

122 *Tyne Wave* (1893-1916 Trawler) 1891 / 121t. Transferred to Aberdeen as A 736. Lost in 1918 off Shetland.

123 *Tynemouth* (1893-1905 Trawler) 1891 / 134t. Sold to the Netherlands.

106 *Tynemouth Abbey* (1927-32 Trawler) 1918 / 202t. Strath class trawler 3764. Transferred to Aberdeen as A 221 *Sunlight*.

128 *Tynemouth Castle* (1928-39 Trawler) 1918 / 202t. Strath class trawler 3765. Foundered on 12th December 1939, no details.

205 *Tyneside* (1895-1907 Trawler) 1895 / 91t. Sank following a collision in 1907, no other details known.

65 *Tynesider* (1889-94 Dandy) 1889 / 69t. Sold to Spain.

1368 *Unity* (1884-85 Paddle Tug) 1866 / 72t. Foundered after catching fire on 24th January 1885.

343 *Ursula* (1902-19 Drifter) 1902 / 72t. Sold to the Admiralty.

314 *Useful* (1904 Sail Lugger) **** / 20t. Ceased fishing.

259 *Valentia* (1898-1919 Trawler) 1898 / 110t. Transferred to Yarmouth as YH 60.

1049 *Vanguard* (1884-87 Paddle Sloop) 1858 / 73t. Ceased fishing.

353 *Vera* (1903-13 Drifter) 1903 / 64t. Vessel lost in 1913, no other details available.

10 *Viceroy* (1899-1913 Trawler) 1899 / 150t. Transferred to Aberdeen as A 598. Lost in conflict in June 1915.

1359 *Victor* (1885-90 Paddle Sloop) 1869 / 71t. Scrapped.

30 *Victoria* (1887-89 Paddle Sloop) **** / ****. Scrapped.

1042 *Victoria* (1884-86 Paddle Tug) 1870 / 140t. Fate unknown.

1287 *Victoria* (1885-86 Paddle Sloop) 1873 / 79t. Later registered as SN 1503.

1503 *Victoria* (1886-97 Paddle Sloop) 1873 / 79t. Ceased fishing.

238 *Victoria Regina* (1897-1917 Trawler) 1897 / 146t. Transferred to Aberdeen as A 590.

242 *Victorian Prince* (1897-1928 Trawler) 1897 / 126t. Transferred to Aberdeen as A 292.

1407 *Victory* (1885-86 / 1892 Paddle Sloop) 1883 / 87t. Later registered as SN 1490. Reverted to registration SN 1407.

1490 *Victory* (1887-91 Paddle Sloop) 1883 / 87t. Reverted to registration SN 1407.

174 *Viella* (1916 Ketch) 1898 / 143t. Lost in conflict on 23rd September 1916, 38 miles SE of Spurn Light.

3 *Violet* (1923-24 Dandy) 1883 / 34t. Ceased fishing.

96 *Wansbeck* (1890-1900 Trawler) 1890 / 60t. In March 1900 the vessel went missing in the North Sea.

1470 *War Cry* (1887-89 Sail Lugger) **** / 20t. Later registered as SN 288.

288 *War Cry* (1901-04 Sail Lugger) **** / 20t. Ceased fishing.

1423 *Washington* (1885-93 Paddle Tug) 1870 / 124t. Reverted to tug duties.

1403 *Water Lily* (1884-85 Paddle Tug) 1883 / 75t. Foundered on 8th March 1885 off Ness Head.

1085 *Waterston* (1881-83 Paddle Tug) 1866 / 72t. Ceased fishing.

1454 *Wellington* (1885-87 Trawler) 1884 / 90t. Sold to France.

200 *Welsh Prince* (1895-1915 Trawler) 1895 / 122t. Transferred to Aberdeen as A 280. Lost on 12th August 1916 after running ashore in fog off the Girdlestone Lighthouse.

86 *Westward Ho* (1891 Trawler) 1890 / 110t. Sold to Brazil.

1360 *Wild Rose* (1882-91 Paddle Sloop) 1874 / 75t. Transferred to Leith.

325 *Wild Rose* (1902-17 Trawler) 1902 / 156t. Transferred to Granton as GN 83.

1119 *William* (1881-84 Paddle Tug) 1865 / 80t. Later registered as SN 1475.

1475 *William* (1887-90 Paddle Tug) 1865 / 80t. Transferred to Hull.

1493 *William Dodds* (1885-1903 Paddle Smack) 1885 / 87t. Ceased fishing.

SN 283 *William H Hastie* – scrapped in 1962.

SN 75 *William King*.

71 *William Ferrins* (1921-25 Trawler) 1918 / 235t. Strath class trawler 3755. Lost on 15th April 1925 off Collieston, Scotland.

1459 *William Findlay* (1887-96 Paddle Smack) 1884 / 87t. Transferred to Aberdeen.

283 *William H Hastie* (1916-62 Trawler) 1916 / 229t. Scrapped.

75 *William King* (1921-57 Trawler) 1918 / 204t. Strath class trawler 3851. Scrapped.

66 *William Osten* (1889-95 Trawler) 1889 / 112t. Transferred to Aberdeen as A 856. Lost in 1909 at Aberdeen.

92 *William Purdy* (1914-54 Trawler) 1914 / 194t. Reportedly sunk in 1954.

209 *William Stephenson* (1895-1903 Paddle Trawler) 1895 / 129t. Transferred to Grimsby.

1422 *William Wouldhave* (1885-98 Paddle Sloop) 1884 / 86t. Renamed *Stag* and transferred to Sunderland.

313 *Windsor Castle* (1902-10 Trawler) 1901 / 183t. Sank following a collision on 13th May 1910.

345 *Wolseley* (1903-17 Trawler) 1903 / 158t. Transferred to Grimsby as GY 1067.

944 *Zenith* (1881-83 Sail Lugger) **** / 37t. Lost off Dieppe, no other details available.

1194 *Zephyr* (1885-91 Paddle Sloop) 1876 / 69t. Lost on 14th November 1891 off Sunderland.

The catch of a single trawler, *T W Irvin*, in the early 1950s.

Doug Darling, John Carr Snr, Hector Makie and Charlie Howard, of the *T W Irvin*, inspect the catch.

Acknowledgements

I am indebted to the extensive help afforded to me by James Cullen Snr, recently deceased, and the continued help of his son James Purdy Cullen for his proof reading, technical assistance and the provision of many of the photographs used throughout this book.

The photograph used for the front cover of this book together with many other photographs were provided by Martin Pontin of William Wights, Provisions Grocer, Fish Quay, North Shields, who has been very supportive. If you ever have the opportunity of visiting this establishment you will not be disappointed by the experience of shopping in a unique setting and with a form of personal service long since lost. These premises were formerly the Highlander Hotel so when you are served your bacon, flour and vegetables you are actually standing at the bar.

The bar of the Highlander Hotel.

The premises as they are today.

I must also pay tribute to the personal assistance, photographs and newspaper cuttings that I have received from the following people: Iris Lacey, Peter Forster, Alan Garner, Margaret Adams, Bob Cawley, Bill and Meg Stephenson and Robert Thompson-Dix.

The assistance and access to records that I have received from the staff at the Tyne and Wear Archives, Blandford Street, Newcastle has been invaluable and the facilities at the local studies centres at North Shields and South Shields Libraries have been useful. I am also grateful for the assistance of the *Fishing News*, Nicola Webb and Jack Davitt in allowing the use of their poems.

The research and information gleaned from the many publications read is shown in the bibliography section.

We should not forget the men who made this book possible and who continue to provide us with fish on a daily basis, often during periods of weather when the majority of us would not set foot outside of our doors never mind going to sea.

Finally I must thank my wife Margaret for her faith and encouragement during the last eight years that this book has taken to research and write.

Ron Wright

Bibliography

British Vessels Lost at Sea 1914-1918, HMSO, London
British Vessels Lost at Sea 1939-1945, HMSO, London
Steam Fishermen in Old Photographs, Colin Elliott
Lost Trawlers of Hull 1835-1987, Alec Gill
Fish 'n' Ships, John Goddard & Roger Spalding
The Numerical Fleet of Yarmouth, L.W. Hawkins
Shipwrecks off the North East Coast Vols 1 & 2, Ron Young
The Organ of North Shields and its Growth, William S. Garson
The County Borough of Tynemouth Police 1850-1969, Internal Publication
Local Wreck Register, No author (South Shields Library)
Warships of World War 1, Ian Allan Publications
Warships of World War II, Ian Allan Publications
British Steam Tugs, P.N. Thomas
The Real Price of Fish, George F. Ritchie
Tynemouth Roll of Honour 1914-1919, County Borough of Tynemouth
Kelly's Directories of Northumberland, Kelly's Directories Ltd

Maitlands Quay, 1914.

The Author

The author, Ron Wright, is a retired Detective Chief Inspector who served in Northumberland County Constabulary, Northumberland Constabulary and Northumbria Police. He lives in Cullercoats with his wife Margaret and has two grown up children, a son Christopher and a daughter Jacqueline.

Although a native of Newcastle, he has had an affinity with North Shields, in particular the Fish Quay since his teenage years and his wife Margaret was born overlooking the Fish Quay.

Following a discussion in his local pub with his friend Brian Atchison (Atchie) over his father's trawler, he decided to research the trawler's history and was surprised to find that very little information was held in the library and little research appeared to have been done regarding the North Shields fishing fleet. As a career detective he was ideally suited to ferret out the facts but he did not expect that it would take eight years to produce a book that he was satisfied with.

Ron Wright could not have achieved his task so thoroughly had it not been for the assistance of Jimmy Cullen Snr who sadly is no longer with us. Jimmy was a rough diamond but a mine of information on all things to do with trawlers from the east coast.

There is no significant memorial to recognise the fishermen of North Shields but hopefully one day someone may help Ron to rectify this!

The author, Ron Wright (right) with Martin Pontin of William Wights.

North Shields Fish Quay, 2002.

The People's History

To receive a catalogue of our latest titles send a large SAE to:

The People's History
Suite 1
Byron House
Seaham Grange Business Park
Seaham
County Durham
SR7 0PY

www.thepeopleshistory.co.uk